FINAL NIGHT

*Precious Truths and
Priority Teachings from Jesus,
Our First Comforter*

Reed D. Tibbetts

FINAL NIGHT
© 2017 by Reed D. Tibbetts

Published by Insight International, Inc.
contact@freshword.com
www.freshword.com
918-493-1718

ISBN: 978-1-943361-24-3
E-book ISBN: 978-1-943361-25-0

Library of Congress Control Number: 2016958588

Printed in the United States of America.

ENDORSEMENTS FOR *FINAL NIGHT*

"I have known my friend, Reed Tibbetts, for thirty-six years. I am convinced that Reed is a man of absolute integrity. He is a diligent student of the Bible. He is comfortable in his relationship with the Holy Spirit. I am anticipating further Biblical teachings from Reed Tibbetts."

—Richard C. Benjamin Sr.,
Apostle and Founding Pastor of
Abbott Loop Christian Center,
Anchorage, Alaska

"Reed serves faithfully and loyally as one of the elders in the church I pastor. He is one of the best theological minds I have had the privilege of calling my friend. His teachings are a unique mix of potent ingredients that form a special recipe of the truth, and reach the minds and spirits of those he teaches. Relax, receive, and enjoy the concepts of his latest book."

—Mike Connaway, Senior Pastor of
VLife Church, McKinney, Texas
and Author of *My Third House*

"Reed Tibbetts is one of the most preeminent theologians I have ever met. He brings his steeped knowledge of the Bible, and uses his God-given anointing, to write books that encourage and challenge all believers to grow in their relationship with God. Reed has a great ability to reach all generations in his writings and teachings. He is truly a man of God."

—Gabriel Kvalvik, faithful member of
the *I Serve* team at VLife Church,
McKinney, Texas

DEDICATION

I dedicate this book "FINAL NIGHT" to my pastor Mike Connaway. His Biblical message of grace as pastor of VLife Church in McKinney, Texas, is so much "of the Holy Spirit," that it has challenged me and increased my faith to do all that the Lord wants me to do.

In November of 2010, my wife and I were faithful members of a large mega church in the Dallas area. The worship and messages were very good, and we were always refreshed by each Sunday. In addition one of our daughters and her family attended, so it always gave us the opportunity to love on the grandkids and compare notes with our daughter and son-in-law. My wife and I had arrived at a unique time in our lives where we were free to move anywhere, and do anything. Don't misunderstand me: we were not and never will be independently wealthy. But I had been unemployed for fifteen months; we had finally sold our home, and were ready to go wherever. More importantly, we had arrived at the point in our lives where we only wanted one thing: to go where God wanted us to go, and do what God wanted us to do, in whatever way He wanted it to be done. There was no more personal agenda or point of pride that mattered. We were ready for what the Lord wanted: Here we are, Lord; send us. We were about to buy our motor home, in anticipation of traveling where the Lord wanted us to go. Besides, we had lived in Texas for five years, and were looking forward to fleeing the Texas heat (we've lived in the Northwest all our lives).

I was cruising around Facebook, and I saw Mike's name. His last name has an unusual spelling and I wondered if it could be someone from my distant past. I shot off a simple email: Are you who I think you are? He responded that he was, and we set up a lunch date to get together. Now let me back up thirty years. I was a staff pastor at a church in Seattle, and there was a young man, recently born again, who began attending that church. My pastoral heart was for young men in the body of Christ, and so I taught and trained whomever I could. I participated in that young man's water baptism and imparted what I could. I moved on in ministry and did not know where he ended up. That young man was Mike Connaway; since then he had been in full time pastoral and coaching ministry for twenty-five years. Back to 2010: Pastor Mike and his wife Lisa had come to Texas to have a central location from which they could travel in the work of the ministry. They were not looking to plant a new church, but the Lord had something else in mind. So He directed them to start a local church and they did so, in obedience to Him. That was VLife Church. Jan and I were looking for a local church to be our covering as we traveled in ministry, so maybe this renewed contact was the Lord's doing. Mike and Lisa instantly agreed to ordain and cover us, so we proceeded with the motor home purchase, and travel preparations. We attended a number of services, and in carefulness and submission to Pastor Mike, were used regularly in prophecy. Just four months later, God directed my wife and me to become part of VLife Church. The Holy Spirit had told me in a crystal clear way to support Pastor Mike. "Lift up his arms." Now for almost five years we have been part of VLife Church, and in submission to Pastor Mike. We serve as elders in the church, and have ministered in teaching, prophecy and prophetic prayer as the Holy Spirit and Pastor Mike have directed.

Mike's pastoral ministry is the most Biblical presentation of God's message of grace that I have ever encountered. It is not "sloppy agape," or "greasy grace." It is flat out the Holy Spirit message of conviction and encouragement that enables everyone to succeed in the Lord Jesus Christ. Mike's message has helped me to be more flexible and open to how the Holy Spirit redeems people, and how I should be teaching and writing and ministering. I am of retirement age, and this has given me the shape and direction of my next decades in the work of the ministry for my Lord Jesus Christ. As I have written <u>FINAL NIGHT</u>, I have seen the powerful expression of grace in all that Jesus said to His disciples that night, and it has increased my spiritual insight into God's grace approach to humanity. Thank you, Pastor Mike.

CONTENTS

WHY THE RISE ABOVE SERIES?

Isaiah 2:2, 3 – The word which Isaiah the son of Amoz saw concerning Judah and Jerusalem. Now it will come about that in the last days the mountain of the house of the LORD will be established as the chief of the mountains, and will be raised above the hills; and all the nations will stream to it. And many peoples will come and say, "Come let us go up to the mountain of the LORD, to the house of the God of Jacob; that He may teach us concerning His ways and that we may walk in His paths." For the law will go forth from Zion and the word of the LORD from Jerusalem.

Micah 1:1; 4:1, 2 – The word of the LORD which came to Micah of Moresheth…And it will come about in the last days that the mountain of the house of the LORD will be established as the chief of the mountains. It will be raised above the hills, and the peoples will stream to it. Many nations will come and say, "Come and let us go up to the mountain of the LORD and to the house of the God of Jacob, that He may teach us about His ways and that we may walk in His paths." For from Zion will go forth the law, even the word of the LORD from Jerusalem.

Matthew 5:14-16 – You are the light of the world. A city set on a hill cannot be hidden; nor does anyone light a lamp and put it under a basket, but on the lampstand, and it gives light to all who are in the house. Let your light shine before men in such a way that they may see your good works, and glorify your Father who is in heaven.

Matthew 28:19, 20 – Go therefore and make disciples of all the nations, baptizing them in the name of the Father and the Son and the Holy Spirit, teaching them to observe all that I commanded you; and lo, I am with you always, even to the end of the age.

John 10:10 – The thief comes only to steal and kill and destroy; I came that they may have life, and have it abundantly.

All of these Scriptures are talking about the church of the Lord Jesus Christ in the last days, describing how people from all nations and people groups will come into the church. It is all about the end times ingathering of people into the kingdom of God and the church of our Lord.

Back in the eighth century B.C., during the reigns of the Kings Ahaz and Hezekiah in the nation of Judah, we had two very different scenarios of what happened to the house of God (the Jerusalem temple). It can be summed up very simply: King Ahaz closed the doors of the house of the LORD (II Chronicles 28:24); King Hezekiah opened the doors of the house of the LORD (II Chronicles 29:3). There were also two prophets (Isaiah and Micah) who spoke identical prophecies about the very last days. Isaiah came from an aristocratic family, while Micah was a peasant farmer: two very different classes, but an identical prophecy from the LORD. This end time prophecy, through shadow and substance, tells the end times church exactly how people will be attracted to and come into the church of the Lord Jesus Christ.

The mountain of the house of the LORD, the mountain of the LORD, the house of the God of Jacob, Zion and Jerusalem are all terms referring to the temple in Jerusalem, where God's presence resided. In the New Testament, the church is the temple of God, for His presence resides inside every person who has accepted Jesus Christ as Savior and Lord. This is what the Old Testament prophecy is saying to the church:

- In the last days the church of the Lord Jesus Christ will be raised above all other religions, philosophies and movements. As it is established as chief among all religions, many people from all nations and all kinds of people groups will come into the church, looking to learn the ways of the LORD and how to walk in His paths. Simply put, there will be a large group of people who will become Christians.

This is what I referred to earlier as the end times ingathering. We want this to happen, and it is clearly the will of God, for He is not willing for any to perish, but for all to come to repentance (II Peter 3:9). So how will the church rise above the hills, that is, the religions, philosophies and movements of the world? The answer is found in the teachings of Jesus during the Sermon on the Mount. The church becomes like a city set on a hill; it can't be hidden. The people in the church will be a light that shines out to all people. We are to shine in such a way that they see our good works and glorify God. Our good works are our very lives: our abundant lives. People will see the abundant lives that we live in Jesus, and come into the church to learn more; they will marvel at the ways of the LORD that give us abundant life, and accepting Christ, they will walk in the same abundant lives that we show them.

We have used many methods to shine forth our light and spread the gospel (T.V., internet, social media, evangelism crusades, door-to-door witnessing, street preaching, picketing, political involvement, etc.) and we spend millions of dollars on those methods. But are we seeing the end times ingathering, with masses of people coming into the church? Certainly not in the United States. So I ask another question: are we living the abundant life in Jesus Christ that shows itself as far superior to other religions, philosophies and life styles? Are the people of the world looking at the people in the church and saying, "Wow! Their lives are far superior to and way above anything we are seeing or experiencing. Let's go into the church of Jesus Christ and check it out!" The answer is no. On a one-to-one scale, there are some individuals who come into the church for this very reason, but not on the massive scale spoken of in the prophecies of Isaiah and Micah.

We, the church of Jesus Christ, need to focus our attention on living the successful, powerful, abundant life that God has for us. In every aspect of life: marriage, child-raising, work, business, finances, physical health, mental health, spiritual dimension, etc., we need to live our lives in such a way that it shines brightly and brings people into the church to check it out. Instead of settling for a so-so or struggling life, and making it to heaven by the skin of our teeth; or being content that we are moral and live stable prosperous lives, we need to live the abundant life that results in many coming into the church. So the books of the "Rise Above" series are all about Christians learning to walk in the abundant life. Rise above, and see the harvest of people coming into the church to learn the ways of the Lord and how to walk in them. Many people will come to Jesus Christ to have the abundant life!

Final Night is a book about God's presence inside of every Christian by the Holy Spirit. The things Jesus taught His chosen the night before He was crucified are vital to a successful, abundant Christian life. Enjoy it, learn and increase your abundant life. Rise above!

INTRODUCTION

Picture what it must have been like to be there when Jesus walked the earth in His public ministry. Two things in particular come to mind when we look back at the disciples who traveled with Jesus during those 3 ½ years.

First, we wonder what it would have been like to be there with Jesus in the flesh: to wake up each morning surrounded by His chosen disciples, and to be there when He talked, when He healed, when He performed His miracles. It would have been wonderful! We would have hung on His every word, and been so built up, into mighty ministers of the gospel. We think it would have been so much easier than it is now. Now we have to believe in Him without having seen Him in person. But if we had been there, living in the physical dimension with Him, it would have been easier to hear Him and to do what He wanted us to do. It's almost like we think His chosen disciples had it easy because of His physical presence. Think about it: there were times when Jesus spent hours just talking to and teaching the Twelve. What would it be like if Jesus appeared to us in the flesh and spent several hours speaking to us? We build it up and think it would have been wonderful, and that having it all in the physical dimension would make it much easier to believe and receive. But it was not as easy as we think it was. Yes it was wonderful and awesome, but it was also overwhelming and extremely difficult.

Second, we speculate on how hard it must have been for His disciples to make the shift to the New Covenant. It is hard for us to identify with them because we have almost 2,000 years of the New Covenant behind us. We are grounded in the New Covenant, we know the New Covenant, we love the New Covenant and we preach the New Covenant. But think about the disciples back in the ending days of the Old Covenant. They had over 1,400 years of the Old Covenant behind them. They were grounded in the Old Covenant; they knew it, loved it and preached it. And then – bam! The cross initiated the New Covenant. We have lived with our New Covenant paradigm for almost 2,000 years. They had lived with their Old Covenant paradigm for over 1,400 years. We would find it incredibly difficult to shift our New Covenant paradigm, even a little, and they weren't just shifting their paradigm a little; they were replacing it with a brand new paradigm: the brand new cross of Jesus Christ New Covenant paradigm!

Even after 3 ½ years of ministry with Jesus; even after teachings and explanations from Him, the disciples still didn't get it. Sure they were starting to understand little bits here and there, but they had not grasped the big picture. Just one day before the Crucifixion, and they were still not getting it. They were not mentally, emotionally or spiritually ready for the new paradigm. And so Jesus spoke to them, taught them and prayed for them that final night. And they became the successful, Spirit-filled leaders of the church of Jesus Christ, spreading the New Covenant paradigm to the world. Let's look at the words and teachings of Jesus, and reap the crop of lessons from…that Final Night.

Chapter One

THE SETTING

On the Isle of Patmos for the Word of God
and Testimony of Jesus

In the latter part of John's life (A.D. 80-95) we know that He spent time in Ephesus, then was exiled to the Isle of Patmos, and then probably taken back to Ephesus. We know that he experienced the vision of the Revelation of Jesus Christ while on the Isle. We don't know for sure where he was when he wrote the Epistles of I, II, III John, and the Gospel of John. But I think he may have penned the gospel while still on the island. So I will go with that assumption.

Present Patmos is a small Greek island in the Aegean Sea. It has a population of 2,998, and has an area of 13.15 square miles. The highest point (Profitis Ilias) is 883 feet above sea level. It is part of the Kalymnos region in Greece. The main communities on the island are Chora (the capital city) and Skala, the only commercial port. There are a couple of other smaller settlements (Grikou and Kampos). The churches are Eastern Orthodox in tradition. UNESCO has designated Chora's historic center, the Monastery of Saint John the Theologian and the Cave of the Apocalypse as World Heritage Sites. The monastery was founded by Saint Christodulos.

The Isle of Patmos in the first century was a rocky island, 30 miles square. It was not a penal colony, or a bad desolate place. It had a harbor and city; also several smaller villages. Prisoners were exiled to the island for magic, witchcraft, prophecy, especially if their activities were perceived as a threat to the government and political powers. Most prisoners had to work in the mines.

The old man had been exiled to the island. It wasn't a prison, but it had taken him out of the mainline community of Ephesus. No travel; no crusading, no preaching; isolated and alone. The government hoped that it would still his voice, and weaken this new age movement. It had now been almost 60 years since Jesus had been executed by crucifixion in Judaea.

He remembered his youth, when he had walked the land of Palestine, as part of the small band that Jesus selected to accompany Him. He had been divinely inspired by Him, and so full of optimism and energy for his people, for his country, for the new message in this new age. He had been devastated when they killed Jesus, and he remembered the despair of the disciples. His own hurting heart, his attempts to comfort Mary, and take her in; and then…Jesus appearing!

He reflected upon the acts of the apostles in the following years; from the powerful infilling of the Holy Spirit at Pentecost, to the extraordinary proclamations of Peter. Ministering at Peter's side had been awe inspiring; the miracles, the crowds coming to believe in the Lord Jesus. And that firebrand Paul! His proclamations of the gospel of Christ had turned the empire upside down. It had all been wonderful, overwhelming, perplexing, and so hard to understand. It was so much bigger than what everyone had thought it would be. It had been staggering just to think that the Jewish people could have their own country again, and be set free from

Romans and Gentiles. Then the message of true freedom was extended to Gentiles...who would have thought it? Now the whole Roman Empire, the whole world government was being overshadowed and eclipsed by the good news of the Lord Jesus Christ!

Those words would be life and health to the next generations of Christians.

Multitudes of the followers of Jesus had been killed; so few of the original leaders were left, and he knew his life on earth was drawing to a close. Looking back at everything that Jesus began to do and teach, he reflected upon that night long ago, when Jesus had taught and exhorted and encouraged the Eleven; the night before He had been arrested, tried and crucified. He had read the new gospel Scriptures, from Matthew, Mark and Luke: they had recorded so many great sayings of Jesus. But he began to recall the many things Jesus had said that final night; things that the others had not written down in their gospels. The Holy Spirit kept reminding him of those words on the final night, and he began to see how important and vital those truths were to understanding what it was all about. Those words would be life and health to the next generations of Christians. They must be recorded, in order that the church could be strengthened for the coming years. All the things Jesus had said on that night long ago began to emerge in his mind as monumental. He took up pen and began to write the words of Jesus down, and like honey flowing from the honey comb, they poured forth! The Holy Spirit sharpened his memory, and like it was yesterday, he heard the words flowing from the mouth of Jesus. In this way the words were recorded, the Scripture of the gospel of John was written, and a major portion of that gospel we now have before us in the vital teachings of…That Final Night.

Chapter Two

I AM GOD!

He who has seen Me has seen the Father

John 13:19, 20 – From now on I am telling you before it comes to pass, so that when it does occur, you may believe that I am He. Truly, truly, I say to you, he who receives whomever I send receives Me; and he who receives Me receives Him who sent Me.

*John 14:7-11 – If you had known me, you would have known my Father also; from now on you know Him, and have seen Him. Philip said to Him, "Lord, show us the Father, and it is enough for us." Jesus said to him, "Have I been so long with you, and yet you have not come to know Me, Philip? **He who has seen Me has seen the Father;** how can you say, 'Show us the Father'? Do you not believe that I am in the Father, and the Father is in me? The words that I say to you I do not speak on My own initiative, but the Father abiding in Me does His works. Believe Me that I am in the Father and the Father is in Me; otherwise believe because of the works themselves.*

Picture this: you meet a unique religious person who so impacts you that you leave your present job and present life, and travel with him. You listen to him, you minister with him and even go out yourself and speak and minister as part of his movement. You see society almost get turned upside down because of him. You see people's lives changed, but you also see many religious authorities oppose him. What do you think? Is he a human phenomenon, or a prophet, or something more? You come to think of him as so special that he may be the son of God. But could you make the leap to believing that he is actually God? Now it is a special final night. You don't know what tomorrow holds, but it doesn't look good. And He has decided that he needs to lock down what you need to accept and believe. That somewhat describes what His disciples were experiencing.

Jesus Christ is called the Son of God to help us better understand the manner of His conception. When the angel Gabriel responded to Mary's question about how she could bear a son, since she was a virgin, he indicated the Holy Spirit would come upon her and she would be overshadowed by the power of the Most High; and for that reason, the holy child would be called the Son of God. The title also refers to His relationship with Father God, within the Trinity. The eleven apostles understood that, as Peter had expressed: "Thou are the Christ, the son of the living God." But it was still a stretch for them to realize that He wasn't just the son of God, but in fact God Himself.

As far as Philip was concerned he hadn't yet seen the Father.

Jesus now pointed out to them the straight truth. They had been seeing Him for 3½ years and they knew Him: what He said, what He did and what He was like. And yet they had not really known Him. Now came the jump. From this very night on they were to realize that they knew the Father, because they knew Him (the Son). Jesus was expressing to them that from the moment of these words being spoken and on into the future they would know the Father, since they had already seen Him. I don't know if any of them caught on to what He was getting at, but Philip spoke up and removed all doubt as to their lack of understanding. "Show us the Father and that should do it." As far as Philip was concerned he hadn't yet seen the Father and wanted the Lord to show them. Jesus gently chides Philip: after all this time, don't you know Me by now? Don't you know that I am in the Father and the Father is in me? Then Jesus states it more clearly: he who has seen Me, has seen the Father. It was crunch time, clutch time, go time, zero hour. Once and for all, the disciples needed to set aside their doubt, confusion and hesitancy, and embrace the deity of Jesus. He is our God! No more tentativeness. Almost 2000 years later, and with the benefit of all the Scriptures, we can look back and see that Jesus Christ is God, but it was not an easy position for them to come to. Yet come to it they must!

In his gospel John clearly pointed out from verse one that Jesus Christ is God.

John 1:1 – In the beginning was the Word, and the Word was with God, and the Word was God.

John 1:3 – All things came into being through Him, and apart from Him nothing came into being that has come into being

John 1:14 – And the Word became flesh and dwelt among us, and we beheld His glory, glory as of the only begotten from the Father, full of grace and truth.

John 8:58 – Jesus said to them, "Truly, truly, I say to you, before Abraham was born, I am.

John 10:30 – I and the Father are one.

John expressed the deity of Christ several times in his gospel. Jesus Christ was the Word. John states it simply. From the beginning Jesus Christ existed as God. He created everything: nothing came into existence apart from Him. In the temple Jesus had a lengthy conversation with a group of Jews who had believed Him. But their belief was not as deep as we may think, because the longer the conversation went on, the more antagonistic they became toward Him. When He made the final "I am" statement, they understood He was equating Himself to the Great I Am (Yahweh).

(Back when God was recruiting Moses to lead the Israelites out of Egypt and into the Promised Land, Moses asked God the question: what shall I tell them your name is? If the Israelites ask me what your name is, what shall I tell them? God said, "I Am that I Am. Tell them I AM has sent you." This is the name Yahweh, also referred to as the Tetragrammaton).

So they took up stones to kill Jesus. Anyone who claimed to be God and was not had to be put to death for blasphemy! Jesus hid himself and went out of the temple. At another time in the temple He was pressed to declare that He was the Messiah. He stated that He and the Father were one, and they understood that He was making Himself out to be God. So again, they took up stones to kill Him for blasphemy. He eluded them and went out of the city. Through the 60 years since the crucifixion of Christ, the church knew and embraced the truth: Our Savior, Jesus Christ is God! John remembered how Christ had taken the time on their final night to nail that down. So he wrote it down in his gospel, so that all would hold on to that foundational truth.

On the final night, Jesus reminded them of His claim to be "I Am." And He further referenced the equality of the Godhead in the process of sending. The Father sent the Son; the Son was now sending the Holy Spirit. Whoever received Jesus was receiving the Father, and whoever would receive the Holy Spirit would be receiving Jesus. He put it this way to further emphasize the unity of the Father, Son and Holy Spirit, and the importance that all people receive God in His fullness.

"Jesus, I recognize, accept and proclaim that You are God. You are the Son of God who died for my sins and you are God the Son, fully God. Thank you Lord!"

Chapter Three

NAME POWER!

Jesus claims to have God's Name!

John 17:6-12 – I have manifested Your name to the men whom You gave Me out of the world; they were Yours and You gave them to Me, and they have kept Your word. Now they have come to know that every-thing You have given Me is from You; for the words which You gave me I have given to them; and they received them and truly understood that I came forth from You, and they believed that You sent Me. I ask on their behalf; I do not ask on behalf of the world, but of those whom You have given Me; for they are Yours; and all things that are Mine are Yours, and Yours are Mine; and I have been glorified in them. I am no longer in the world; and yet they themselves are in the world, and I come to You. **Holy Father, keep them in Your name, the name which you have given Me,** *that they may be one even as We are. While I was with them, I was keeping them in* **Your name which you have given Me;** *and I guarded them and not one of them perished but the son of perdition, so that the Scripture would be fulfilled.*

John 17:25, 26 – O righteous Father, although the world has not known You, yet I have known You; and these have known that You sent Me. And I have made Your name known to them, and will make it known, so that the love with which You love Me may be in them and I in them.

Here in this prayer to the Father, Jesus states clearly that He has shown the Father's name to His followers. But what name? There is no indication in the Gospel Scriptures that Jesus expressed the Old Covenant name (Yahweh) to His disciples. He referred to Father God as Father, and he referred to Himself as Jesus and Christ. As He prayed, Jesus was asking the Father to keep them in the Father's name. The Bible teaches strongly that God's name is very powerful and important. Throughout Scripture we are encouraged to invoke God's name over His people, and repeatedly the prophets called upon God to act on behalf of His people because they had His name called over them. Here Jesus was calling on the Father to keep, guard, protect, and provide for His followers, in His name and for the sake of His name!

But what name? Jesus answers that in the prayer. He states clearly that the name the Father gave to Him is the name of the Father. The name of God the Father is the same as the name of God the Son. The name of God the Son is the Lord Jesus Christ. When in the end every knee shall bow and every tongue confess, they will be confessing the Lord Jesus Christ (Philippians 2:10, 11).

Unity update. Jesus petitions the Father to keep His followers in His name, and He ties their unity to being kept in the name of the Father and Son. In this day and age there are so many Christians doing so many different things and saying so many different things, that we almost lose track of how crucial it is that we be unified. There are so many arguments, divisions, criticisms and finger pointing of Christians toward other Christians. We have almost lost our way, and certainly we are not pressing into being unified, just as the Father and the Son are one. Take a walk on the internet wild side and you will see Christian leaders criticizing, name calling and attacking other Christian leaders. We must set aside our pride, prejudice and divisions, and embrace one another. Our unity as Christians is made possible because Father God keeps, guards, protects and provides for us in the name of the Lord Jesus Christ!

During His ministry time on earth, while Jesus was with the disciples, He was keeping, guarding, protecting and providing for them in the Father's name, the name that He had given to Jesus. What name did the Father give to the Son?

Matthew 1:21 – you shall call His name Jesus, for it is He who will save His people from their sins.

Luke 1:31 – and you shall call His name Jesus.

Luke 2:11 – for today in the city of David there has been born for you a Savior, who is Christ the Lord.

Acts 2:36 – God has made Him both Lord and Christ – this Jesus whom you crucified.

What name? The name of the Lord Jesus Christ!

Jesus tells the Father that He made His name known to His followers, and He would continue making it known to them. What name? The name of the Lord Jesus Christ!

*John 14:13, 14 – **Whatever you ask in My name, that will I do**, so that the Father may be glorified in the Son. If you ask Me anything in My name, I will do it.*

*John 16:23-27 – In that day you will not question Me about anything. Truly, truly I say to you, **if you ask the Father for anything in My*** *name, He will give it to you. Until now you have asked for nothing in My name; ask and you will receive, so that your joy may be made full. These things I have spoken to you in figurative language; an hour is coming when I will no longer speak to you in figurative language, but will tell you plainly of the Father. In that day you will ask in My name, and I do not say to you that I will request of the Father on your behalf; for the Father Himself loves you, because you have loved Me and have believed that I came forth from the Father.*

Jesus knew that some of His followers (us maybe?) would get all convoluted about how to ask God for help. Jesus wants us to see the simplicity of asking God in His name, to move on our behalf. He did not want us to get bogged down in the "exact words and procedures" to use to navigate the Godhead (do we ask the Son, in His name, and then He asks the Father, and then the Father will do something?). The moment we ask in His name, the fullness of the Godhead hears us and responds to us: Father, Son and Holy Spirit.

Throughout the Bible God has established a unique and powerful connection to His name. I am speaking of both His connection to His name, and our connection to His name. The connection: God links the calling of His name to the unleashing of His volitional power. And He commands us to release His volitional power by calling His name!

When I attended a Bible college back in the 1970s there was a time when one of the older denominational leaders talked to us about a journey he made long ago to South America. I do not remember when he went there, or what country he went to. I do remember it was a short visit, meeting with missionaries and denominational leaders there. He did not remember who he met, or what was said. But he did remember feeling that he was not accomplishing much for God's kingdom. On his last day there, he persuaded one of the local leaders to go with him in a small boat up a river that went back into the thick jungle, to see if they might encounter one of the native Indian tribes. This had not been done before, and he was told that it wouldn't do any good, because even if they did run across some of the Indians, the language barrier would prevent communication of the gospel, and could result in dangerous circumstances. And so they traveled for several hours up the river. They were about ready to turn around, when they came upon a small clearing, and saw a small village and a few people moving about. Beaching the boat they walked into the village, encountering blank stares from the people there. Repeated attempts at communicating, from both sides, failed again and again. It looked like nothing could be accomplished for the sake of the gospel. Then he noticed an older woman, who was bent almost double from back malformation. He got her attention and began pointing up toward the heavens and repeating one word: "Jesus! Jesus! Jesus!" As the woman listened she began repeating: "Jesus. Jesus. Jesus." Suddenly she straightened up, fully functioning, and showing not a trace of the malformation that had her bent almost double. God had healed her! Shortly thereafter the two men returned to their boat to travel back down river to civilization. The last thing they saw as they drifted away was the woman, standing straight, pointing strongly to the heavens and shouting: "Jesus! Jesus! Jesus!" That story still burns in my heart these many years later, as evidence that God responds to the calling of His name with the release of His volitional power – divine power – supernatural power!

What do I mean by God's volitional power? Simply this: God has volition, just as we do, and with His free will He can choose to do something, just like we can choose to do something with our free will. Scripture teaches that when we invoke God's name, He freely chooses to release His power on our behalf. God says, "I hear you calling My name, and I now choose to release My power on your behalf!"

Now let me use a little sandwich psychology here (+ - +). In the name of the Lord Jesus Christ we are kept, guarded, protected and provided for. That's great! For His name's sake, we will be persecuted (John 15:21). That's not so great. But in the midst of any and all circumstances we are instructed to ask for things (whatever is needed in the moment) in His name, and He will provide. He promised us that whatever we asked for in His name, He would do it. Jesus will do it! The Father will give it! In the name of the Lord Jesus Christ!

"Lord I thank you for keeping me, protecting me and providing for me. I proclaim and call Your name, Lord Jesus Christ, over my life and ministry. Use me, Lord; for Your Kingdom, for Your church and for Your righteousness. I ask this in Your name, Lord Jesus Christ!"

Chapter Four

PARACLETE

The Holy Spirit as Advocate and Counselor

*John 14:16,17 – I will ask the Father, and He will give you **another Helper** (paraklatos), that He may be with you forever; that is the Spirit of truth, whom the world cannot receive, because it does not see Him or know Him, but you know Him because He abides with you and will be in you.*

John 14:25, 26 – These things I have spoken to you while abiding with you. But the Helper, the Holy Spirit, whom the Father will send in My name, He will teach you all things, and bring to your remembrance all that I said to you.

*John 15:26 – When the Helper comes, whom I will send to you from the Father, that is the **Spirit of truth**, who proceeds from the Father, He will testify about Me, and you will testify also, because you have been with Me from the beginning.*

John 16:7-15 – But I tell you the truth, it is to your advantage that I go away; for if I do not go away, the Helper will not come to you; but if I go, I will send Him to you. And He, when He comes, will convict the world concerning sin and righteousness and judgment; concerning sin, because they do not believe in Me; and concerning righteousness, because I go to the Father and you no longer see Me; and concerning

*judgment, because the ruler of this world has been judged. I have many
more things to say to you, but you cannot bear them now. But when
He, the Spirit of truth, comes, He will guide you into all the truth; for
He will not speak on His own initiative, but whatever He hears, He will
speak; and He will disclose to you what is to come. He will glorify Me,
for He will take of Mine and disclose it to you. All things that the
Father has are Mine; therefore I said that He takes of Mine and will
disclose it to you.*

As John the Beloved reviewed in his mind all the things Jesus
had said about the Holy Spirit, he realized the very simple and
straight forward truth: that every Christian needs to have a
full and intimate relationship with the Holy Spirit that is
inside each one. Yet it seems that we Christians through
hundreds of years have made it all way too complicated.
Church leaders through the ages have wanted to guard and
protect all Christians from bad teaching (doctrine); yet that
has sometimes resulted in the complications of things: way
too much complication.

One particular doctrinal issue that complicated things has
been referred to as the Filioque Controversy. (Filioque references the concept phrase "from the Son.") From the 4th
century on through almost 700 years, leaders within the
church taught, fought and disagreed with regard to this
Controversy. I have read so many things about this dispute
that my eyes are crossed from the effort. This issue was one
of the main reasons that the Catholic Church split from the
Orthodox Church.

The Filioque refers to a statement inserted into the Niceno-
Constantinopolitan Creed (A.D. 381). In the second phrase
of the creed concerning the Holy Spirit, leaders of the western
church inserted "who proceeds from the Father and the Son."
This was an attempt to support trinitarianism and reject

certain "oneness heresies." Oneness heresies were false teachings that weakened or denied the Trinity doctrine: that God the Father, God the Son and God the Holy Spirit are one eternally co-existent God.

Over the next 500 years this controversy resulted in disagreements, divisions and excommunications all over the eastern and western regions of the church. It seemed to me that there was a lot of convoluted thinking as to the roles of the Father, Son and Holy Spirit: which member of the Godhead did what, and which didn't do the other's role.

In A.D. 879 the Greek church leaders (eastern church) formally rejected the Filioque statement and made it an important dogma in the Orthodox Church that the Holy Spirit proceeds from the Father, not from the Father and from the Son.

A.D. 1054 is cited by most as the time that the Catholic Church formally split into the Roman Catholic Church (western region) and the Eastern Orthodox Church (eastern region). The three main issues that split the church were: which bishop would be the leading bishop for the whole church (bishop of Rome or bishop of Constantinople); whether images (icons) should be used in worship; and finally this Filioque Controversy. The following phrases from the gospel of John address the issue:

John 14:26 – But the Helper, the Holy Spirit, whom the Father will send in My name...
John 15:26 – When the Helper comes, whom I will send to you from the Father...
John 16:7 – but if I go, I will send Him to you...

It is stated clearly that both the Father and the Son sent the Holy Spirit to us. As I read about this controversy, I began to feel like someone who was arguing over how many angels can dance on the head of a pin. That argument does nothing to further God's kingdom, God's righteousness and our personal relationship with Him. It also reminded me of the "partyism" that Paul referred to in I Corinthians chapter one.

I Corinthians 1:12, 13 – Now I mean this, that each one of you is saying, "I am of Paul," and "I of Apollos," and "I of Cephas," and "I of Christ." Has Christ been divided? Paul was not crucified for you, was he? Or were you baptized in the name of Paul?

Paul was exhorting the Corinthian church to avoid divisions. As I read over the many arguments and reasonings behind the Filioque Controversy, it seemed to me that Christians were trying to make "parties" out of the Godhead: "I am of the Father; I am of the Son; I am of the Father and the Son; I am of the Holy Spirit." There is no "partyism" or division within God. From eternity to eternity, God is God; through creation, covenants, the Cross and the Church Age, the Father, the Son and the Holy Spirit were there, are there and will always be there. As we consider what Christ said about the Holy Spirit on that final night, let's remember the simple truth that John remembered: Every Christian needs to have a full and intimate relationship with the Holy Spirit that is inside each one. He knew that our closeness to His Spirit within enables, empowers and equips us for the successful Christian life. Let's review the words of our Lord on that final night, and use them to strengthen our relationship with God.

The church lost its 501(c)(3) tax-exempt status with the IRS.

The Holy Spirit is our Helper.

The Greek word (paraclatos, paraclete) is translated variously as comforter, helper, counselor, advocate, etc. Literally it means called to the side of, for the purpose of help. In those times it would have been used for the counsel for the defense. But more than a defense lawyer, it would be like a friend who is helping and advising the defendant. Early in my ministry, I was presented with an unusual opportunity. The church, at which I had just become a staff pastor, had recently lost its 501(c)(3) tax-exempt status with the IRS. I was asked to review the correspondence and get our exempt status back. It was a thick file because a previous staff pastor had communicated a lot with the IRS. Once I had reviewed everything, I realized that it was a misunderstanding. Our representative had provided the IRS with a flood of information, without adequate explanation of some transactions. I have learned that when working with the IRS, less is better. I composed a careful, one page letter that addressed the circumstance, corrected the misunderstanding, and outlined the path to our re-instatement as a tax exempt organization. Just before I sent the letter, we (the church leadership) submitted it to a tax attorney for his review. He said it looked fine, but suggested the addition of one sentence. I followed his advice and inserted the sentence. The letter was sent, along with prayer, and we waited. About three weeks later, we received a letter from the IRS that simply thanked us for the clarification, and re-instated our tax exempt status. Praise the Lord! I share this tale to simply show that the tax attorney I consulted was like an advocate that had fuller knowledge and experience with what the IRS needed to hear (hence the added sentence). In a similar way the Holy Spirit, our Helper, is our spiritual specialist and friend. He is the one who is called to our aid;

the one who appears in our behalf; our mediator, our inter-cessor, our helper. The Holy Spirit is our personal advisor, agent and representative.

Before we go any further, I want to point out that the Holy Spirit is "another" Helper. Jesus Himself is our Helper. In I John 2:1 the word is used of Jesus Christ: "And if anyone sins we have an advocate (helper) with the Father, Jesus Christ the righteous." So we can say that Jesus is our Paraclete and the Holy Spirit is also our Paraclete. The things that the Holy Spirit does for us are the things Jesus was doing for His disciples, as He walked this earth.

So the things that Jesus did for His followers while He walked this earth, the Holy Spirit now does for us. Jesus taught them; He bore witness of the Father, and He convicted and convinced them of all things right and wrong. The Holy Spirit, who is inside every Christian believer, now carries on the "Helper" work that Jesus was doing. Another Helper.

The Helper convicts and convinces the world of sin, right-eousness and judgment. You may find it uncomfortable that I discuss the Helper convincing and convicting the world. After all isn't his help and advice for Christian believers, and not for the world? Let's take a closer look at that. First and foremost before we became Christians we were part of the world. And God so loved the world that He gave his only begotten Son. God wants every person in the world to come to repentance, experience salvation in Him and not perish. The Helper loves and wants to help every person, Christian and non-Christian.

1 — Sin really means to miss the mark; to miss the target.
Everyone does things where we miss the mark. Jesus Christ is the only human who made it through His life on earth

without missing the mark. In our hearts, every one of us wants to overcome our sin; our falling short; our missing the mark. But how? The Helper works to convince every person that the only way to overcome sin is to believe in Jesus Christ. That's the convicting power of the Helper. The people who walked the earth with Jesus, but did not believe in Him, still had the Helper trying to convince them of the need to believe in Jesus, even after the crucifixion. The Helper just keeps working with people, convicting and convincing them with regard to sin.

2 — **Righteousness refers to doing the right thing and being in the right position.** The Helper works to convince people of what is right and how to be in the right position in Jesus Christ. Jesus was doing this very thing throughout His ministry on earth. When Jesus was killed, resurrected and ascended into heaven, the Helper kept right on working to convince people of the right things to do.

3 — **Judgment refers to the appropriate consequences for actions taken.** The ruler of this world (Satan) has already been judged, cast out of heaven because of his rebellion and pride. The Helper does not want any human to suffer the same fate, so He works to convince us that there are consequences for what we do, and He wants us to choose the right, to choose to believe in Jesus, to receive the gift of salvation and the right position in Him.

The convicting and convincing work of the Helper is provided for all, so that every person can understand wrong actions, right actions and the consequences. Don't be deceived by Satan: whatever a man sows, that shall he also reap. Allow the Helper to be your friend and advisor. Let Him convince you.

The Holy Spirit is our Spirit of Truth.

As God, the Holy Spirit knows everything. He is eternal, and knows all truth, past, present and future. Jesus said of Himself, "I am the way and the truth and the life." So too, the Holy Spirit is the truth: our Spirit of Truth.

Let me wander for a moment. As a man who loves worship, and a worship leader for many years, I have found the Holy Spirit to be the key to higher worship. Jesus said that true worshippers should worship the Father in spirit and in truth. The Holy Spirit, inside of us, aligns our spirit with Him and the truth and enables us to worship in spirit and truth. When I have strived to lead people into higher worship, and it just doesn't seem to be happening; if I let go of my striving, hug the Spirit and let Him hug me, open my awareness to the believers around me, and then begin to express love and thanks to the Father, we enter a higher plane in the spiritual dimension. And it is thick and powerful and wonderful! Let God's Spirit embrace you; wrap your arms around Him and ascend into higher praise and worship. Try it, you'll like it. And the Father positively loves it!

1 — The Spirit of Truth teaches us all things. It would be easy if the Spirit of Truth would schedule a 1-hour session with us at the beginning of each morning, and audibly teach us everything we needed to know for the day. But it doesn't work that way. Even when Jesus (who is God) gave instruction to his followers, they misunderstood some of what He said. It's almost like we need to be spoon fed, a little at a time, in order to understand and receive. I have been a committed Christian for 46 years, and the Lord still teaches me a little at a time. It works best that way. The beauty of it is that I have the Spirit of Truth inside of me, and at the right moment he feeds me the spoonful of instruction I need.

One more thing before I move on. He teaches us all things. I simply believe that all means all. He doesn't just teach me the "heavenly" things. He teaches me whatever it is that the moment and the circumstances require. Have you ever been on the job, working on some problem, and needing help in figuring out the solution? You may think because it has nothing to do with the church, or the spiritual realm or ministry, that God is not concerned about it. But He is involved in every part of your life. Ask the Spirit of truth for the work situation answer, and He will help! He instructs according to the need of the moment. Every need; every subject; every circumstance: Now that's phenomenal!

2 — The Spirit of Truth brings to our remembrance all that Jesus has ever said to us. As Jesus was speaking so much to His followers that final night, He knew that they would have trouble remembering it all; yet alone all the things He had been speaking to them for 3½ years. So He gave them the assurance that the Spirit of Truth would remind them of everything He had said to them. I'm in my 60's now, and I have found that I'm not as sharp as I used to be, in quoting a Scripture, or recalling something that I had memorized in the past. They call it "senior moments"; as if only senior age people forget things. But my friend, the Spirit of Truth, who lives inside of me, does help my recall of God's Word. God's Word falls into the category of all that Jesus has said to me. There have also been distinct times when God has spoken a personal word to me; not in an audible voice, but a voice heard by my soul and spirit. Those personal words also fall into the purview of the Spirit of Truth, and his "recall" ministry to me. It works like this: when we need recall of specific words or Scripture from God, the Spirit of Truth recalls it to our memory, according to the need of the moment. That too is phenomenal!

3—The Spirit of Truth guides us into all the truth. He guides in the sense of leading and guiding us ever deeper, into all the truth. When an ocean-going ship nears the Panama Canal, a special pilot must be taken on, to lead and guide the ship deeper into the complicated Panama Canal passage. The passage (48 miles long) is one of those unique situations where the master of the ship must turn control of his ship over to someone else. To get a picture of the challenge, think of yourself behind the wheel of a 50-ton Cadillac that is around 900 feet long. The road is icy, your brakes are mushy, and you have to put your car into a parking place with just a few feet of clearance on the sides. Sounds impossible, doesn't it? It takes at least 8½ years to become fully qualified to handle any of the many vessels that transit this Panama Canal waterway. These pilots put in long hours and 13-hour shifts are not uncommon. Yet canal pilots are relaxed and self-assured.

Perhaps it is because of the years of experience they have traversing the canal passage. They have the knowledge and the experience to go deeper into the canal. It takes eight to ten hours to make the trip. When it is completed they turn the ship back over to the master, and take a ride on a motor launch to shore. So too, the Spirit of Truth is our guide to take us deeper into all the truth. He guides deeper, according to the need of the moment. Wow!

Here is that word again: "all" the truth. Once again I will say that I believe that all means all. He doesn't just guide me into deeper "heavenly" truth. The next time you lose your keys, remember that they are usually in the last place you left them. Can't remember? Well the Spirit of Truth knows where they are. I know you may think it sounds silly, but ask Him. What do you have to lose?

4—The Spirit of Truth discloses to us what is to come. To disclose is to reveal by declaring. The Spirit of Truth knows everything past, present and future. Knowing the future He will declare to us what's coming, when we need to know it beforehand. He absolutely can tell the future because He knows it, but this does not mean that He becomes our fortune teller. We almost always want to know things before they happen, but God knows when we need to know the future, and He will disclose and declare it to us, as needed. I am glad we can trust the specific knowledge of future things to the hands of the Spirit of Truth. Every time that He does declare what is to come, it's a thrill and a blessing because we learn of it at the perfect time. Thank you, Lord!

5—The Spirit of Truth discloses the things of the Father and the Son to us. Jesus has made it clear that He and the Father are one, and His followers need to know that this new person of the Holy Spirit (new to them, but eternally co-existent with the Father and Son) is not a different god. Everything the Spirit of Truth says and does is exactly what the Father and Son are saying and doing, and want to be said and done. There's no different angle; no different road that leads to the same destination. No variation on the same truth. Every time we try to somehow relate "individually" to one of the persons of the Godhead, we fail to understand that the Lord our God is one God: Father, Son and Holy Spirit. I have heard it taught that we are in the dispensation of the Holy Spirit, which followed the dispensation of the Son, which followed the dispensation of the Father. There are times I am uneasy with that language because it may focus on one person of the Godhead, to the exclusion of the others. From creation through the Old Covenant times, through the Church Age, God the Father, God the Son and God the Holy Spirit are all equally present. The Holy Spirit will always reflect the words and actions of the Father and Son, and never individualize Himself to us.

The reality that God in His fullness would be in His people was new.

From the day of the Crucifixion to the Day of Pentecost was about 50 days, and during that time everything was put in place for the moving forward of the New Covenant in Jesus Christ. Jesus addressed the circumstances, staging and sequence of the covenant transition: from Old Covenant to New Covenant, by specifying that the Spirit of Truth was with the disciples, but would be in them. The reality that God in His fullness would be in His people was new, and Jesus was clearly setting the stage for them: to wait in Jerusalem until the Day of Pentecost and receive power with the baptism of the Holy Spirit. From crucifixion to resurrection, to ascension and into the Holy Spirit coming upon them and baptizing them, the New Covenant reality of having God inside of each and every Christian came into reality. The Spirit of Truth moved from abiding with them to actually being in them. Phenomenal!

The Holy Spirit is our...Holy Spirit!

He is holy – perfect, righteous and set apart. And He is spirit – functioning fully in the spiritual dimension. We are spiritual beings in that when we accepted Jesus into our hearts and lives, our spirit was born again. We live and move and have our being in the spiritual dimension through our spirit, and the Holy Spirit is our personal guide and protector in the spiritual dimension. Our perfect God is within us, and is our guarantor of wholeness, success and confidence in the spiritual realm.

1—The Holy Spirit bears witness of Jesus Christ. The single, most significant event in the pattern of human history is the cross of Jesus Christ. Everything Father God said and did, prior to the Crucifixion, was designed to lead up to the death of Jesus. With every step that He took, and every word that he breathed, Jesus pointed to His own death on the cross. The plan of salvation by believing in and accepting salvation through the death of Jesus on the cross, is a plan that the Godhead designed, pointed to and produced. So it continues in the Church Age and by the Holy Spirit, we bear witness of Jesus Christ. The Holy Spirit does this continually, and He is really good at it. Sometimes we aren't so good at bearing witness, but help is at hand: the Holy Spirit, inside of us, bears witness! We just need to talk to people about what Jesus has done for us, and the Holy Spirit helps us with the words and sentences. If we listen to Him, He helps our very attitude, vocal intonations and subject content, so that people are lovingly and tenderly drawn to Jesus. This is such sweet teamwork!

2—The Holy Spirit glorifies Jesus Christ. Salvation in Jesus is so important that we can't say too much to lift Jesus up, to praise Him, to bring attention to Him, and to glorify Him for doing the most important thing that could have been done for the human race!

3—The Holy Spirit does not speak on His own initiative, but whatever He hears (from the Father and Son) He speaks to us. It has been interesting to watch people bring focus and attention on to God the Holy Spirit, the third person of the Godhead. Whether it was the Pentecostal movement in the early 20th century, the Latter Rain movement of the 1950's, or the charismatic movement of the 1960's, there were people who focused so strongly upon the Holy Spirit and the manifestations of the Spirit, that it almost gained primacy over the atoning work of Jesus on the cross.

An illustration of that: In the 1970's I had the privilege of attending many services in Pentecostal and charismatic churches. I consider myself a Pentecostal and a charismatic, but with a bent toward decency, order and edification in all things. I remember visiting a congregation in Washington State. They had recently completed a new auditorium, which included a great water baptismal tank at the back center of the platform. Over the baptismal hung a beautiful white dove, representing the Holy Spirit. In the Bible when Jesus was baptized in water by John the Baptist, the Spirit of God did descend upon Him in the form of a dove, as the Father spoke: "This is my beloved Son in whom I am well pleased." But in the church building? Every church I had seen, up to that point in my life had a cross at the center of their platform, but not this church. That pastor and congregation wanted everyone to know that they desired the fullness of the Holy Spirit in everything they did. I made no comment, but my spirit, and the Holy Spirit within me, said that it just wasn't right. The Holy Spirit is all about Jesus and the cross. He is a perfect gentleman, who speaks to us, again and again, the things that the Father and the Son say. There's no 3rd person of the Godhead agenda; there's no charismatic focus. Every gift, every word, every spiritual thing is focused, like a laser, on salvation and the cross of Jesus. That is what the Holy Spirit is all about!

With the Holy Spirit to teach us and guide us into all the truth, as the Spirit of Truth; and to convict/convince us of sin, righteousness and judgment, as the Helper; and to keep our "laser focus" on salvation for anybody through the cross of Jesus; we can participate in an intimate relationship with the 3rd person of the Godhead. We have a tendency to regard the Holy Spirit as an object (baptism with the Holy Spirit, power of the Holy Spirit, gifts of the Holy Spirit), when we should relate to Him as our personal God. God the Father, God the Son, and God the Holy Spirit are God: personal, loving and desirous of a personal relationship with us.

"Spirit of God, it is so special that You are inside of me; You love me so much, and You help me with everything. You keep me on track, and guard me against distractions, side tracks and rabbit trails. I am going to call you Spirit, but not in some esoteric way, but as my friend. Thank you, Spirit, for being my close, personal friend and keeping me on target!" I just love the Paraclete!

Chapter Five

DIRTY FEET

Do you know what I have done to you?

John 13:1-4 – Now before the Feast of the Passover, Jesus knowing that His hour had come that He would depart out of this world to the Father, having loved His own who were in the world, He loved them to the end. During supper, the devil having already put into the heart of Judas Iscariot, the son of Simon, to betray Him, Jesus, knowing that the Father had given all things into His hands, and that He had come forth from God and was going back to God, got up from supper, and laid aside His garments; and taking a towel, He girded Himself.

John 13:5 – Then He poured water into the basin, and began to wash the disciples' feet and to wipe them with the towel with which He was girded.

John 13:12-17 – So when He had washed their feet, and taken His garments and reclined at the table again, He said to them, "Do you know what I have done to you? You call me Teacher and Lord; and you are right, for so I am. If I then, the Lord and Teacher, washed your feet, you also ought to wash one another's feet. For I gave you an example that you also should do as I did to you. Truly, truly, I say to you, a slave is not greater than his master, nor is one who is sent greater than the one who sent him. If you know these things, you are blessed if you do them.

Throughout Bible times, from Abraham and Lot to Jesus and John, foot washing was a common custom. In first century Judea, they didn't wear shoes and socks, but open-strapped sandals. Anything that a person walked through, kicked up or stepped in got onto the sandals and onto the surface of the skin. You can see why it was common custom to wash the feet when you first came into a dwelling. Foot washing was for cleanliness and comfort. Homes at the time were mostly made of stone and mud bricks. Depending upon the economic level, poorer homes were single level. On that one level when you first entered, there would be a dirt floor area, where domestic animals would be kept, and then the family area, which was often raised slightly on a platform. People who were better off had two levels, and the upper room was kept cleaner and often for special circumstances. The roofs were for storage and, when it was hot, people would sometimes sleep there. In those first century times, it was the custom for the feet to be washed when people first entered the house. Provision for foot washing was considered to be appropriate hospitality to show to a guest. The usual action was for the homeowner to provide basin, water and towel for the visitor to wash his own feet. In more affluent homes, it was customary for servants to wash the feet of the guest. If you understand how dirty and smelly feet could become, you can see why this task fell to the low-ranking servants. It was considered degrading, disgusting and humbling for the servant. When Peter visited the house of Simon the Pharisee, Simon neither offered water to do the task, nor had servants perform it for Jesus. That's why the sinful woman was so humble in crying and washing the feet of Jesus with her hair and tears. Simon showed no humility; the woman showed complete humility (Luke 7:36-47). And so we come to the final night, and John chapter thirteen. From the other gospels, we know that an unnamed benefactor provided a large upper room for Jesus to be with His disciples for the Passover meal. It is interesting that nothing is said about foot washing before they had all entered the upper guest room and began partaking of the meal. We know that amongst the Twelve, there was some rivalry as to who outranked whom, and who would be first (under Jesus, of course). Perhaps none were willing to take the role of a servant; not even for their own feet. It would be hard to believe that their feet were not dirty, since they had been staying outside of Jerusalem, and they walked into the city to arrive at the upper room location. Now let's take a closer look.

The Scripture indicates that Jesus had total self-awareness, self confidence and self destiny on this final night. He knew that His hour had come to depart out of the world and go to the Father. From Matthew 16:21 we know that Jesus was aware of the things He was about to suffer. He also knew that the Father had given all things into His hands. What does that mean? Jesus had the authority to submit to or refuse to submit to the Cross! He knew that He had come forth from God and was going back to God. Jesus flat out knew that He was God, and He knew that He was returning to the position of top authority in the spiritual dimension (the heavenlies – Ephesians 1:20, 21). I say it again: Jesus had total self-awareness, self confidence and self destiny. From that position He now taught self-sacrifice and service.

Jesus loved His own: the Twelve Disciples who were with Him, including Judas. His love was unconditional and was to the end. He wanted each of them to know and embrace the essential truth of servant-hood. So while supper was still going on, He got up, took off an outer garment, tied the rest of his clothes up tight, put water into a basin and began washing their feet, and drying them with a towel. You have to put yourself in their places to imagine how strongly this action slapped them into astonishment, awareness and awe. Peter erupted against Jesus doing this, but finally submitted into silence. Yes, you could hear a pin drop. Jesus got back up, put his outer garment back on, and reclined back at the table. And He said:

"Do you know what I have done to you?"

His question was rhetorical. You can imagine all the disbelief and guilt they were feeling. Jesus had to take them beyond the guilt and astonishment. He had to get them thinking of the true reason for His actions: not to shame them, but to set them free: free to serve. He pointed out that they had come to know and understand that He was their Teacher and Lord. If He could wash their feet, then surely they could wash one another's feet. Not only could they serve one another, but they should! He proved Himself to be the servant example: if He had done it, they were to do it. They had all kinds of reasons for holding back from being humble servants of one another: position, authority, ignorance, jealousy, pride. They had all kinds of thoughts: That's not my job. That's not my duty. That's not my ministry! I heal people....I cast out demons....I preach the gospel....I serve the Master! I sit next to Jesus.

It's not for me to take the lowliest position.

It's not for me to take the lowliest position. All of that reasoning and thinking was flushed in this moment. Jesus said, "A slave is not greater than his Master." I am the Master: you are the slaves. I am the One who sent you out to proclaim the gospel and to perform miracles. But you are not greater than Me: I am the Sender and you are the sendees. Serve one another. Serve one another. Serve one another! If you get hold of this truth and do it, you are blessed. Prove that you have really heard what I am saying, by really doing it!

A number of years ago, a young lady shared a story with me that illustrates the heart of the servant. This young lady loved the Lord, and loved the denomination that she was a part of. Her father was a simple country pastor in that denomination, and she loved him and appreciated her upbringing and heritage in the Lord. She had gotten a position working in the national headquarters for that denomination, and was exposed to larger city churches, and a new level of professionalism and polish in the work of the Lord. There came a time when the national meeting for the denomination took place. Her father hadn't always been able to come to the national meetings, due to distance and expenses, but she realized that if he came and stayed with her, he would be able to afford it. Best of all, he would be able to see her work, and the bigger picture of the big city and the bigger churches. She received special assignments to coordinate the schedule and events of the national meeting. She so wanted her dad to see her work and be proud of her efforts and position. Now it was important that she be early to every event to make sure everything flowed smoothly. Her father had a habit that seemed to be getting in the way of her schedule. They would travel together each day to the meetings, and her dad always seemed to be stopping and talking to strangers. Five minutes here, five minutes there, and it was making her late! On the third day they were heading to a main event in a downtown building, and as usual her dad had stopped a couple of times to talk to strangers. They got into the elevator to get up to one of the higher floors for the main event. Her dad began talking to a stranger in the elevator. When they got to the proper floor, he was still involved in deep conversation with the man. Exasperated, she stepped out of the elevator and had to wait for a couple of minutes until her father finally stepped out of the elevator. She couldn't hold her peace. "Dad, you've made me late to take care of the beginning of the meeting, and this is very important to me and to everyone at denominational headquarters. Things have to go just right. What were you taking so long to talk to that man about?" Her father stayed silent for a long moment. Then he said, "I'm sorry sweetheart. That man was at a crisis in his life, and I was able to lead him in accepting Jesus as his Savior." She was speechless. In that moment she realized how unimportant her "details" and tasks were, in comparison to the vital conversations her dad had been having with strangers. She realized her position was so important to her that she was not responding to the needs of everyday people. Who was serving?

The tools of a Christian are the basin and the towel. What is the need of the moment? That is the very thing that a Christian needs to do, to be the kind of servant Jesus wants us to be: meet someone's need of the moment! These days we don't use the terms servant, slave or service. We've dressed them up somewhat talking about our ministry, our ministers, our callings. That's OK, but we need to be servants. That's what His kingdom and His righteousness is all about. Like Jesus, we need to have total self-awareness, self confidence and self destiny. It is often our insecurity that results in us grasping for our position. Be aware that you are a child of the King, a joint heir with Jesus Christ and you are the righteousness of God in Him. When you embrace your true identity and position in God, you are confident, not insecure. And you can carry out your destiny: self-sacrifice and servant-hood that benefits others. I am a servant and slave of the Master of the Universe!

Chapter Six

LOVE COMMANDED?
LOVE DEMANDED?

By this all men will know

John 13:34, 35 – "A new commandment I give to you, that you love one another, even as I have loved you, that you also love one another. By this all men will know that you are My disciples, if you have love for one another."

John 14:15 – If you love Me, you will keep My commandments.

John 14:21-24 – He who has My commandments and keeps them is the one who loves Me; and he who loves Me will be loved by My Father, and I will love him and will disclose Myself to him. Judas (not Iscariot) said to Him, "Lord, what then has happened that You are going to disclose Yourself to us and not to the world?" Jesus answered and said to him, "If anyone loves Me, he will keep My word; and My Father will love him, and We will come to Him and make Our abode with him. He who does not love Me does not keep My words; and the word which you hear is not Mine, but the Father's who sent Me.

John 15:12-14 – This is My commandment, that you love one another, just as I have loved you. Greater love has no one than this, that one lay down his life for his friends. You are My friends if you do what I command you.

John 15:17 – This I command you, that you love one another.

Can love be commanded? There are times that we talk about romantic love like it is an involuntary condition of our emotions that we can't help or control. "I can't help it, daddy. I love him!" There are other times when we describe love as something each individual chooses to do, or not. "Nobody can tell me who I have to love. You can't make me love someone. It's my choice." The Lord did create each of us with free will. He wants us to choose to do the right thing. But He does not hesitate to help us see what is right by commanding us. When He knows that we have chosen Him, He also knows that our desire is to know and do what He wants us to do. So He does not hesitate to give us commands; thus emphasizing important things.

A Commandment to Love – The New Commandment

On the final night, just before He was to be arrested and crucified, Jesus gave a commandment to His disciples. He called it a new commandment because He really wanted their attention and focus. Throughout His ministry with them, He had taught them to love everyone: to love their God, to love their neighbor and to love their enemies. But now He was focusing their attention on their internal relationships. Love one another. The love expressed by Christians for Christians is such a crucial concept that Jesus called it "new." It wasn't an old commandment or an enhanced commandment: it was a new commandment. Over the last 50 years, I have owned a lot of cars (maybe twenty-four between my wife and me). I have had old bangers, old reliable, used but good, almost new, and yes, sometimes new! I am thankful for every car that the Lord provided. But there was something about a new car that made me focus, sit up and listen: a beautiful sound, a fantastic smell, and it looked so good. When Jesus said "A new commandment," the disciples sat up, focused and listened.

He also gave it as a commandment (Greek-entola), an order. As an army combat medic, I learned the difference between discussion, suggestion and an order. I had a double chain of command. Through the Headquarters Company, my medical staff sergeant and captain were my superiors, but in the field my infantry company sergeant and lieutenant were my superiors. So when a firefight broke out and the sergeant yelled a command, I obeyed it. At the same time he could care less what my hair looked like in the jungle. When we returned to the firebase for three days, and my medical staff sergeant told me to get a haircut, I got a haircut…it was an order. When Jesus said to them, "Love one another," the verb he used was an imperative: a command. But in addition to commanding them, He called it a commandment. If I paraphrased it I would say: "I command you this command: Love one another!" Paul gave us good insight into this new commandment when he wrote in Galatians 6:2: "Bear one another's burdens, and thereby fulfill the law of Christ." Several years ago a theme moved through the church: the "one another" gospel. It embraced every Scriptural concept of successful, loving relationships in the church. "Love one another" is the foundation of the one another gospel.

An Example of Love – The Perfect Example

Jesus pointed to His loving of His disciples as the example from which they could draw the picture of how they were to love each other. "Just as" means "in the same way." Now when we are told to be just like Jesus, we sometimes get discouraged, because He was and is spotlessly perfect. And when Jesus said that He loved them just as Father God loved Him, that could also seem like an insurmountable goal. How can we possibly love one another just like God the Father and God the Son loved each other? If we take a more practical approach to actions of love, we can accept and be inspired by the challenge. Rather than being discouraged by thinking you can't be as good as God, think in the sense we have heard so many times in the last few years: What would Jesus do? To paraphrase, Jesus was saying: "Look at the things I have done for you; at the way I have talked with you: that's the way I want you to act in love toward one another." We see another picture of this comparison concept in Ephesians 5:25: "Husbands, love your wives, just as Christ loved the church and gave Himself up for her,..." Jesus is the example for every Christian husband: to give himself up for his wife. And He is the example for every Christian, in how to love each other, even to the extreme sacrifice.

John 15:13 – Greater love has no one than this, that one lay down his life for his friends.

Romans 5:7, 8 – For one will hardly die for a righteous man; though perhaps for the good man someone would dare even to die. But God demonstrates His own love toward us, in that while we were yet sinners, Christ died for us.

I have had the privilege of seeing men put their lives at risk for others in the battle situation. I was an army combat medic in Viet Nam and Cambodia. There came a particular day when one of our squads was ambushed while on patrol. I had to go out to help the wounded, and was shot myself. I wanted to quit, and just lay perfectly still so no one could see me or shoot me again. But I crawled around anyway, to help other wounded men. I saw men come out of safe positions to help us. I remember vividly Ketola, our 60-machine gunner coming out and laying down a steady stream of fire, so that other men could come into the open to grab us and carry us to safety. I remember Private Hill grabbing me in a man-carry, and running across an open field to get me back to safety. Men risked their lives that day, trying to help others live; two died. Jesus Christ demonstrated His love for His disciples by choosing to lay down his life on the Cross. "Love one another, just as I have loved you."

A Way to Love – Tangible and Timely

John 13:1 – Now before the Feast of the Passover, Jesus knowing that His hour had come that he would depart out of this world to the Father, having loved His own who were in the world, He loved them to the end.

John 14:21 – He who has My commandments and keeps them is the one who loves Me; and he who loves Me will be loved by My Father, and I will love Him and will disclose Myself to him.

When we get close to the final accomplishment of our goal; when we finally see the end in sight, we want to carry out the final act; and finishing up all the long stretch details sometimes falls along the wayside. After all, it's the final goal that is really important, right? A few years ago, I received a promotion from a sales manager in Oregon, to a plant general manager in Texas. It was a goal I had worked toward for several years. I had to travel back and forth a couple of times as I took care of closing details at the old plant, while direct-ing preparatory details at the new plant. It was very difficult to make sure that every last thing got taken care of at the old plant, so no balls got dropped; it was made more difficult because my heart was at the new plant. I was responsible for the new plant's P&L (monthly profit and loss report) two months before I actually made the move. It was only because I believe in the Biblical mandate (to do my work heartily, as unto the Lord, for it is the Lord Christ that I serve) that I managed to nail down every last little thing. It was one of those rare times in my employment life that I carried out every little detail to the end.

So much of the doctrine of the Deity is given to them on that final night.

Jesus knew that the ultimate goal of His coming in the flesh was about to happen: the cross and salvation for all who would receive it. Knowing that, He loved them to the end. He focused every part of his being onto His disciples. That final night He spent hours talking, teaching and encouraging them; to prepare them for the cross and the church. Jesus disclosed Himself to them. So much of the doctrine of the Deity is given to them on that final night. Everything He was disclosing to them about Himself would help them understand and walk in the New Way. Knowing more about Christ was preparing them for the cross and the church. He was doing this because they loved him and had kept His commandments, and He loved them and revealed Himself to them.

A Proof of Love – Keep My Commandments

In John chapter fourteen Jesus moved beyond the new commandment to love one another, into the greater realm of

His commandments (plural). He stated the equation both ways: If you love Me, then you will keep My commandments. If you keep my commandments, then you love Me.

God's thoughts and ways are far above our thoughts and ways. When we have someone telling us what to do, we quickly jump to questioning and judging their motives. "Who are you to try and tell me what to do?" or "If you loved me, you wouldn't make me do that." That's human, but that's not God. The Lord wanted the disciples to be set free from the wrong mentality about God and about fulfilling His commands.

There are people that we obey out of fear. A wife obeys an abusive husband because she fears being beaten. An employee does what the boss says because the boss threatens to fire him, and he fears losing his job. In a similar way, some people obey God's commandments out of fear: fear of what God might do to them. But God is not a God of fear, and He does not want our obedience out of fear. God is not going to beat you or throw you out, if you slip up and don't obey. The grace of the cross covers our sins; past, present and future.

There are people who obey God in order to be seen righteous, and earn their way into God's good graces. If I do enough of what God wants me to do, He will give me goodies. Or even worse, there are those who believe that God must reward us if we do certain things, so we can control Him, like our sugar daddy. But God is not a God of "salvation by works" or "prosperity by works." He does not want us to be motivated by desire (or lust or greed) for rewards.

God understands that when we love Him, our obedience will flow freely. He wants us to have the comfort and beauty of our love for Him. "Come to Me, all who are weary and heavy-laden, and I will give you rest. Take my yoke upon you and learn from Me, for I am gentle and humble in heart, and you will find rest for your souls. For My yoke is easy and My burden is light." (Matthew 11:28-30). Wearing His yoke and carrying the load that He wants us to carry is good for us. It may sound like work, but He knows what is best for us, and so you can say that it is a yoke of love and a load of love. We can relax in our love relationship. His love for us is the ultimate "trust" relationship, and we are set free to love Him and obey Him.

As we keep His commandments out of our love for Him, both Father God and God the Son will make their abode with us. To make their abode with us is pretty strong language that carries with it the meaning of dwelling together long term. It's not just a visit once in awhile, it's living together like a family lives together long term. That's love. Let's keep His commandments out of love and experience the depths of His love.

The Result of Love — All People Will See

Along with Jesus, we want to be a witness to everyone in the world, so that all will have the opportunity to receive Christ as Savior and Lord. We witness by our words and by our deeds: what we say and what we do. Jesus knew that if His disciples truly loved one another, everyone who saw them would know they were disciples of Christ. But with all things that humans touch, it seems that the picture people see is often not a picture of Jesus. Over the years there have been divisions and disagreements that have resulted in denomination after denomination. Humans latch on to all kinds of things in order to discriminate and divide: nationality, race, economics, social grouping, sin grouping; all to separate and divide. And at times, it seems the church is no different. When I look at all the companies and corporations I have experienced; when I

consider all the organizations I have observed and participated in; when I examine all the churches I have seen and
been a part of; it has all been about the same with regard to
division and discrimination. The Lord Jesus Christ wants His
church to be so much more! We are to be the salt of the earth
and the light of the world; we can't be that when we squabble,
but we can be that when we love one another like Christ
commanded us.

Many years ago I heard someone say that the Christian army
is the only army that shoots its own wounded. Now, as I surf
the internet, as I view Face book, as I listen to the radio, I
experience grief over the criticisms and complaints that
Christians post about other Christians. Christians attack one
another just like academicians do, just like political leaders do.
In the name of accountability and often through the use of
"open letters," Christians are criticized, without regard to
God's pattern of brother-to-brother communication. To the
world the church looks just like any other human organization. God's heart hurts over this.

*I Corinthians 1:10-13 – Now I exhort you, brethren, by the name of
our Lord Jesus Christ, that you all agree and that there be no divisions
among you, but that you be made complete in the same mind and in
the same judgment. For I have been informed concerning you, my
brethren, by Chloe's people, that there are quarrels among you. Now
I mean this, that each one of you is saying, "I am of Paul," and "I of
Apollos," and "I of Cephas," and, "I of Christ." Has Christ been
divided? Paul was not crucified for you, was he? Or were you baptized
in the name of Paul?*

*I Corinthians 11:18, 19 – For, in the first place, when you come together
as a church, I hear that divisions exist among you; and in part I believe
it. For there must also be factions among you, so that those who are
approved may become evident among you.*

Paul expressed clearly that divisions among Christians and the Church are unacceptable. If there are divisions, there is only one acceptable purpose: so that we know who and what are approved. When that becomes evident there should be no more division. God wants us complete in the same mind and the same judgment. Jesus calls us back to the new commandment: Love one another. The more we do that, the more the world sees that we are different from all the human organizations of the world; that we are disciples of the Lord Jesus Christ, the one true God. In the words of John the Beloved: "Beloved, let us love one another."

God commands it and we need to demand it of ourselves: LOVE ONE ANOTHER!

Chapter Seven

SERVANTS AND SLAVES

Set free to serve

John 13:16 – Truly, truly, I say to you, a slave is not greater than his master, nor is one who is sent greater than the one who sent him.

Jesus had just finished washing the disciples' feet. We know that amongst the Twelve, there was some rivalry as to who outranked whom, and who would be first (under Jesus, of course). It seems that none of the disciples were willing to take a servant's role and wash feet; not even for washing their own feet. As I have said before: it would be hard to believe that their feet were not dirty, since they had been staying outside of Jerusalem, and they walked into the city to arrive at the upper room location. So Jesus washed their feet. "Do you know what I have done to you?" You can imagine the guilt they were feeling at seeing the Master do what they weren't willing to do. Jesus had to take them beyond that guilt: He had to get them thinking of the true reason for His actions: not to shame them, but to set them free: free to serve.

John 15:15 – No longer do I call you slaves, for the slave does not know what his master is doing; but I have called you friends, for all things that I have heard from My Father I have made known to you.

We are slaves to one another, because more than anything else, we need to serve one another. When Jesus said he would no longer call them slaves, He was not canceling His commandment that they should serve one another. Rather He was showing the new depth and knowledge of their relationship with Him. As His friends, He had made known to them all the things the Father had told Him. He no longer held back information from them. As the New Covenant was being established in the cross of Christ, He wanted them to have a deeper "friendship" relationship with Him. They needed that relationship and all that knowledge to carry forth the gospel through the first century. I might paraphrase it like this: "You need to be slaves of one another; and more than that, I have made you My close friends, so that together we can reach the world, as I build My church."

John 15:20 – Remember the word that I said to you, 'A slave is not greater than his master.' If they persecuted Me, they will also persecute you; if they kept My word, they will keep yours also.

Jesus indicated that the world hated the disciples, just as they hated him. When they experienced that hatred from some, He wanted them to remember that the world had also hated Him. Something had happened to the disciples. As Jesus chose them out of the world for the new and higher purpose of proclaiming the gospel to all, they were no longer like the world. And the world hated them because of that. Knowing that this kind of hatred and persecution would be coming to His disciples, Jesus reminded them that the world would relate to them in the same way it related to Him. He wanted them to be encouraged and to take courage from this fact. The world will relate to you in exactly the same way it relates to Me; for good or bad.

John 12:26 – If anyone serves Me, he must follow Me; and where I am, there My servant will be also; if anyone serves Me, the Father will honor Him.

I need a man who can follow directions and do the job well, without questioning everything.

I was told a story many years ago. A man, who had been unemployed for many months, was looking for any kind of job that would feed his family. He was interviewed by a man who owned a construction company. The owner asked, "Will you do what you're told to do?" The man eagerly responded: "Yes, sir!" So the owner decided to give him a try. He told him to report for work the next morning at 8:00 am sharp. When he arrived, he was told to report directly to the owner. The owner took him out into an old warehouse. Against the south wall of the warehouse was a huge pile of bricks. It looked like they had been there for a very long time: all dusty, dirty and scattered around. "Take all these bricks and put them against the opposite wall." So the man spent all day, moving bricks with a wheel barrow. Even though they had been in a messy pile, he carefully stacked them against the north wall. By the end of the day he was quite tired, but satisfied that the job was done. "Come back tomorrow morning at 8:00 am sharp." So the next day he was there on time, and told to report directly to the owner. The owner took him out to the old warehouse, and looked over the neatly stacked bricks on the north wall. He didn't say a word, but he took the new employee over to the west wall and said, "Take all the bricks from the north wall and put them against the west wall." This seemed kind of weird to the new employee, but he didn't say a word; instead he just got the wheel barrow and spent all day moving bricks from the north wall to the west wall, once again stacking them neatly. When the day was done, the job was finished. He went home tired, but happy that he was earning a paycheck. He had been told once again to report the following morning at 8:00 am sharp. He was not surprised when he was directed to the owner the next morning. They went out to the old warehouse, and once again the owner inspected the neatly stacked bricks on the west wall, without saying a word. He took the employee back to the empty south wall and said, "Put all the bricks back on the south wall." The employee felt bewilderment and some irrita-tion. But he thought to himself, "The boss is the boss." So he spent another day with the wheel barrow, moving bricks from the west wall and stacking them against the south wall. His muscles were sore this third day and he was grateful to reach the end of the day, just finishing in time. He went home and fell in to bed for a stiff and solid sleep. When he reported for work the next morning at 8:00 am sharp, he was sent straight to the owner. The owner said, "I've been out to the warehouse to inspect the bricks on the south wall. They looked good. I want you to take a position as my new operations manager, beginning today." The new employee sat bolt upright and said, "I accept! Thank you so much!" Then he paused and asked, "What was all the brick moving about?" The owner simply said, "For my operations manager, I need a man who can follow directions and do the job well, without questioning everything. You proved you could do that." In the same way, Jesus wants us to serve Him by doing what He says to do (follow Me!), and doing it well. Jesus wants us following Him and being with Him. As we serve Him in this way, Father God honors us, with provision, protection and power.

John is thinking about servants and slaves

Mark 10:35-45 — James and John, the two sons of Zebedee, came up to Jesus, saying, "Teacher, we want You to do for us whatever we ask of You." And He said to them, "What do you want Me to do for you?" They said to Him, "Grant that we may sit, one on Your right and one on Your left, in Your glory." But Jesus said to them, "You do not know what you are asking. Are you able to drink the cup that I drink, or to be baptized with the baptism with which I am baptized?" They said to Him, "We are able." And Jesus said to them, "The cup that I drink you shall drink; and you shall be baptized with the baptism with which I am baptized. But to sit on My right or on My left, this is not Mine to give; but it is for those for whom it has been prepared." Hearing this, the ten began to feel indignant with James and John. Calling them to Himself, Jesus said to them, "You know that those who are recognized as rulers of the Gentiles lord it over them; and their great men exercise authority over them. But it is not this way among you, but whoever wishes to become great among you shall be your servant; and whoever wishes to be first among you shall be slave of all. For even the Son of Man did not come to be served, but to serve, and to give His life a ransom for many.

So John is thinking back. It's been many years, but he is remembering the things Christ said that final night about serving. And he remembers something that happened earlier, when he and his brother were feeling their oats, and wanted to pre-empt the other disciples and secure high positions in the kingdom they thought Jesus was establishing. They wanted to be second only to Jesus. They even used their mom to prepare the way with Jesus. I cannot help but think that John was feeling some shame and regret. Since this episode was recorded in both the gospels of Matthew and Mark, it wasn't like it was a deep, dark hidden secret. I'm certain that many Christians who knew John had read these gospels. So they knew what he had done at an early age. John had long ago reconciled with his Lord, and moved beyond this early mistake. But as he reviewed what Jesus said on the last night about servants, he also remembered what Christ had said after that earlier incident. His disciples were not to pursue lording it over others; they were not to make it their goal to be "great" or to be the "first" in the kingdom. Instead they were to be servants of one another and slaves of all. Two words are used here by Christ to express service in the kingdom of God.

Diakonos

To be great in God's kingdom, be a servant (diakonos) to one another. This Greek term literally meant "one who serves table." It could be in an inn (we would refer to them as waiters/waitresses at a restaurant) or at a wealthy man's table. It was often used of a public official (like we would say "public servant"). In the Jewish community, when this term was used, it carried with it some semblance of dignity. It was for dignified, higher purpose service. It could refer to a freeman or it could be used of a servant who was owned by someone else, but if it was, they were viewed as nobler than common slaves.

Doulos

To be first in God's kingdom, be a slave (doulos) of all. This term referred to a bond-servant, owned by someone else. This slave was viewed by the Greeks and the Jews as a lower form of humanity. He could own nothing. Even his own wife and children were not his own. His master owned them (if that sounds like something right out of black slavery in the deep south of the United States before the Civil War, then you are getting the right idea). For Jews it was considered one of the worst insults if you called a freeman a "doulos." One could be sued and punished for slander by calling someone else this word.

Jesus wanted his disciples to serve one another and to serve mankind, with all the dignity stripped away; with complete selflessness. We serve Jesus; we are owned by Jesus, and ministering in the kingdom of God is all about selfless, lowly service, and not about greatness or "firstness" in any way, shape or form. That's what Jesus does.

Chapter Eight

UNITY - INDWELLING

The presence, peace and protection of God always within us

Under the Old Covenant, during Old Testament times, God spoke of dwelling among His people, with His presence represented in the tabernacle or temple, especially in the inner Holy of Holies. But under the New Covenant, which began when Jesus died on the cross and continues through today, God actually dwells in His people; we are His temple/tabernacle and His presence is inside of us. This is referred to as the indwelling presence of God. It is fantastic because it is the presence, peace and protection of God, always within us. On this final night of instruction, Jesus weaved His indwelling presence into and through our unity as Christians.

*Romans 8:10, 11 – If **Christ is in you,** though the body is dead because of sin, yet the spirit is alive because of righteousness. But if the Spirit of Him who raised Jesus from the dead **dwells in you,** He who raised Christ Jesus from the dead will also give life to your mortal bodies through His **Spirit who dwells in you.***

In the letter from Paul to the Romans, God indicates that Christ is in us through His Holy Spirit indwelling us, giving our spirit and our body life. Paul also mentions this concept in his letters to the Corinthians (I Corinthians 3:16, 17; 6:19; II Corinthians 6:16). So the indwelling presence of God in each Christian was an accepted and taught concept thirty years into the development of the New Testament church. Sixty years into the New Testament church experience, John looked back to the Final Night, and remembered how Jesus spoke of the indwelling.

John 14:16-20 – I will ask the Father, and He will give you another Helper, that He may be with you forever; that is the Spirit of truth, whom the world cannot receive, because it does not see Him or know Him, but you know Him because He abides with you and **will be in you.** *I will not leave you as orphans, I will come to you. After a little while the world will no longer see Me, but you will see Me; because I live, you will live also. In that day you will know that I am in My Father, and you in Me and I in you.*

Jesus spoke of the Holy Spirit being with them, and soon in them. He was referring to the fact that the moment He died on the cross, everyone who believed in Him would have the Holy Spirit come to live inside of them. He then spoke in all encompassing language: He said that in that day they would realize that Jesus was in the Father, and that they (the disciples) were in Jesus, and that Jesus was in them. I have heard it said that Father God is in the throne room of heaven, Jesus is also there at the right hand of the Father, and the Holy Spirit is inside each Christian believer (all of that is true). So it is said that we need to relate to the Holy Spirit and speak to Him because He is the One within us, while the Father and the Son are in heaven (that is not true because it wrongly separates the Godhead). Jesus was trying to help His disciples understand that the fullness of God would be in them, and on that day they would know this and better understand it.

John 15:4, 5 – Abide in Me, and I in you. As the branch cannot bear fruit of itself unless it abides in the vine, so neither can you unless you abide in Me. I am the vine, you are the branches; he who abides in Me and I in him, he bears much fruit, for apart from Me you can do nothing.

When Jesus spoke to them about their fruit-producing ministry, He emphasized that they needed to abide in Him, and that He would abide in them. To abide means to live in, to stay in something in the same way as one would stay in their home. Jesus Christ lives inside of us, and we need to live inside of Him!

*John 17:20-23 – I do not ask on behalf of these alone, but for those also who believe in Me through their word; that they may all be one; even as You, Father, are in Me and I in You, that they also may be in Us, so that the world may believe that You sent Me. The glory which You have given Me I have given to them, that they may be one, just as We are one; **I in them and You in Me**, that they may be perfected in unity, so that the world may know that You sent Me, and loved them, even as You have loved Me.*

God the Father, God the Son and God the Holy Spirit are in us.

Jesus stated it in several different ways. In the New Covenant we would have God living inside of us: the Father, the Son and the Holy Spirit. Then, just before He went out with His disciples and He was arrested, He concluded the Final Night teachings with a prayer to His Father. Even in this prayer He was teaching His followers more truth. He prayed earnestly for the disciples present with Him, and for all who came after and believed in Jesus because of what the disciples said and taught (figure it out: that includes you and me!). He prayed for their unity: that they would all be one. He gave us the glory of the Father and Son so that we could have unity just like the Father and the Son are unified. Then He expressed the crucial connection: Jesus is in us and the Father is in Him. This is the indwelling presence of God in us. God the Father, God the Son and God the Holy Spirit are in us. That is the key that perfects us in unity. On our own and through our own well-intentioned efforts we can have a lot of agreement and even come into some unity. But eventually our human efforts will fall short, and we will create division and practice prejudice toward one another. That's not unity or agreement at all. So how can we be unified? The answer is in the indwelling presence of God. If and when we first tune in to God inside of us, then our divisions and prejudices become meaningless. God inside each and every one of us works to perfect our unity: that we may all be perfected in unity.

John 17:26 – and I have made Your name known to them, and will make it known, so that the love with which You loved Me may be in them, and I in them.

It is the love of the Father for the Son, and because of the love of the Son for us, that God in His fullness indwells us. And as we connect with and focus on God within us, we come into perfect unity.

I have watched a number of recent TV shows, and read a number of fiction books in which a team of several people have to work together to pull off the perfect crime, or the perfect sting, or the perfect arrest, or whatever. And they have a most interesting technical device. They call it an earwig or ear bud. Apparently this has been improved so much that it is clear inside the ear and no one can see it. Some of them even portray some kind of implant. With these implants or ear buds every member of the team can hear one another, and any support staff back at the office or in the airplane or wherever, can hear everyone. They are able to coordinate their actions to accomplish their task. It's really cool as you watch it or read about it. It's kind of like a souped up Mission Impossible. Well, the indwelling presence of God can be like that, if we allow it to be. If each one of us will first tune in to God within us, listen to Him, and then reach out to one another, it will be amazing what we can agree on and what we can accomplish for the kingdom of God. Picture the ministry and success of the church as we move forward in perfect unity: one Lord, one faith, one baptism. "Lord, perfect us in unity and send us forth to victory!"

So on that final night Jesus earnestly wanted to implant the right concept in His followers. He wanted them to have the unity that He Himself shared with Father God. And He wanted them to understand that complete agreement and perfect unity was possible, if they would take advantage of the indwelling presence of God that they would have. So he expressed it from every angle, so that they would come to see that Jesus was inside of them, that the Father was inside of them, that the Holy Spirit was inside of them. He then expressed why it was so important that they worked through His indwelling presence to come into unity. It would be a testimony to the world that Father God had sent His Son Jesus Christ to die for their sins and provide salvation. Our unity is the shining light that shows the gospel of Jesus Christ to the world. Let's tap into God inside of us, and in unity and agreement share the light and truth of the gospel with every-one, so that all who come to repentance will be saved!

Chapter Nine

TRAITOR

Even Jesus was betrayed

A Chosen One

*John 6:70, 71 – Jesus answered them, "Did I myself not choose you, the twelve, and yet **one of you is a devil?**" Now he meant Judas the son of Simon Iscariot, for he, one of the twelve, was going to betray Him.*

Judas…Judas Iscariot…the name has rung through the ages, crying out, "Betrayal!" We find the story very poignant. There came a time in the earthly ministry of Jesus that He selected twelve men from His many disciples for special train- ing and assignment. He named them as apostles with the responsibility of carrying the gospel message to the world. He taught this inner circle special things and passed on to them special knowledge. Judas was one of these Twelve. The perfect God-man, Jesus, had one of His special apostles turn on Him and betray Him to His enemies. You and I have prob- ably had times in our lives that people that we trusted turned on us, and it was a disappointment. But imagine that one of your very top lieutenants turned on you and made a deal to have you arrested and killed. That's what happened to Jesus.

A Perfume Anointing

John 12:4-6 – But Judas Iscariot, one of His disciples, who was intending to betray Him, said, "Why was this perfume not sold for three hundred denarii and given to poor people?" Now he said this, not because he was concerned about the poor, but because he was a thief, and as he had the money box, he used to pilfer what was put into it.

Matthew 26:14-16 – Then one of the twelve, names Judas Iscariot, went to the chief priests and said, "What are you willing to give me to betray Him to you?" And they weighed out thirty pieces of silver to him. From then on he began looking for a good opportunity to betray Jesus.

Luke 22:3, 4 – And Satan entered into Judas who was called Iscariot, belonging to the number of the twelve. And he went away and discussed with the chief priests and officers how he might betray Him to them. They were glad and agreed to give him money. So he consented, and began seeking a good opportunity to betray Him to them apart from the crowd.

About a week before the Passover and the Final Night of instruction and prayer, Jesus was having supper in Bethany at the home of Mary, Martha and Lazarus. Martha was serving the meal, Lazarus was reclining at the table with Jesus, and Mary proceeded to anoint the feet of Jesus with a costly perfume of pure nard. She was actually wiping His feet clean with her hair. Judas protested that it was a waste of money, but Christ corrected him, indicating that what Mary was doing was symbolically honoring Him prior to His burial. We don't know what Judas was thinking: maybe he was realizing that Jesus was not going to lead a revolt and establish an earthly kingdom; maybe he was thinking that the funds he had been stealing were going to dry up. Whatever was running through his mind, this "perfume" event was a turning point, and he decided to split with Jesus and seek his fortunes through another channel. Judas was a thief, and the question he asked the chief priests was not, "What should I do?", but instead, "How much will you pay me to betray Jesus?" That says something about his character.

The Unclean One

John 13:10, 11 – Jesus said to him, "He who has bathed needs only to wash his feet, but is completely clean; and you are clean, but not all of you." For He knew the one who was betraying Him; for this reason He said, "Not all of you are clean."

Jesus had just finished washing the disciples' feet, including the feet of Judas.

Jesus had just finished washing the disciples' feet, including the feet of Judas. Jesus knew that Judas was in the process of betraying Him, and yet the lesson He was teaching them about washing one another's feet and serving one another was so important that He wanted them to remember for all time that He had washed their feet, including Judas. Looking back at this event they could see that Jesus knew His betrayer before the feet were washed. The other point clearly made is that Judas was not clean. His betrayal of Jesus made him unclean. The Old Testament Law and the traditions of the Jews were all very clear: touch not the unclean! The expected thing to do was to have no contact whatsoever with Judas. But Jesus was teaching them a new thing regarding the unclean. Jesus served the disciples by washing their feet, even though eleven were clean and one was unclean. And He directed them: So also you should wash one another's feet, even if someone is an unclean betrayer. Talk about loving your enemies!

No Blessing for Judas

John 13:18 – I do not speak of all of you. I know the ones I have chosen; but it is that the Scripture may be fulfilled, 'He who eats My bread has lifted up his heel against Me.'

Psalm 41:9 – Even my close friend in whom I trusted, who ate my bread, has lifted up his heel against me.

Jesus promised that His followers who served one another would receive special blessing for their humble service, and He had chosen them for this. But that blessing was not for Judas, because not only was Judas not serving in humility, he was acting against the Lord by betraying Him. Jesus refers to Psalm 41:9 as prophetic of the opposition and abandonment that Judas was performing, while still gathering with the apostles and sharing meals with them. Judas was pretending to be loyal and faithful, even though he had already put his treason into action.

The Betrayer Revealed

John 13:21-30 – When Jesus had said this, He became troubled in spirit, and testified and said, "Truly, truly, I say to you, that one of you

*will betray Me." The disciples began looking at one another, at a loss
to know of which one He was speaking. There was reclining on Jesus'
bosom one of His disciples, whom Jesus loved. So Simon Peter gestured
to him, and said to him, "Tell us who it is of whom He is speaking."
He, leaning back thus on Jesus' bosom, said to Him, "Lord, who is it?"
Jesus then answered, That is the one for whom I shall dip the morsel
and give it to him." So when He had dipped the morsel, He took and
gave it to Judas, the son of Simon Iscariot. After the morsel, Satan
then entered into him. Therefore Jesus said to him, "What you do, do
quickly." Now no one of those reclining at the table knew for what
purpose he had said this to him. For some were supposing, because
Judas had the money box, that Jesus was saying to him, "Buy the
things we have need of for the feast"; or else, that he should give something to the poor. So after receiving the morsel he went out immediately;
and it was night.*

*Luke 22:21, 22 – But behold, the hand of the one betraying Me is with
Mine on the table. For indeed, the Son of Man is going as it has been
determined; but woe to that man by whom He is betrayed!"*

John remembered vividly when Jesus had declared that one of
them would betray Him. Peter himself had gotten him directly
involved in the revealing! From Luke chapter twenty-two, we
see that Jesus had just completed sharing the first communion
with the disciples, before making the statement about a
betrayer. The room was large enough, and the men spread
out enough that it was difficult to hear exactly what was said.
So Peter got John's attention, since John was sitting very
close to Jesus. Peter asked John to find out who He was
talking about. So John, the youngest of them asked Jesus:
"Who is it, Lord?" Jesus indicated that He would dip a
morsel and give it to the betrayer. So He gave it to Judas and
told him to go and do it quickly. Judas knew in that moment
that his pretension of being faithful and loyal had not worked,
and that Jesus knew about his betrayal, so he quickly left.

Some of the apostles did not hear what was said, so they didn't know why Judas was leaving, and certainly did not know that he had been revealed as the one who was betraying Jesus.

Betrayed in the Garden

John 18:2, 3 – Now Judas also, who was betraying Him, knew the place, for Jesus had often met there with His disciples. Judas then, having received the Roman cohort and officers from the chief priests and the Pharisees, came there with lanterns and torches and weapons.

Mark 14:44-46 – Now he who was betraying Him had given them a signal, saying, "Whomever I kiss, He is the one; seize Him and lead Him away under guard." After coming, Judas immediately went to Him, saying, "Rabbi!" and kissed Him. They laid hands on Him and seized Him.

Quite a military presence to arrest this preacher from Nazareth!

Jesus took His followers and crossed the Kidron ravine to a garden area. This was a place that Jesus often brought His disciples, and Judas knew it well. So Judas came to the place with a large contingency. There were officers from the chief priests and Pharisees, and a Roman cohort. Usually a Roman cohort had 600 men, but perhaps the commander had sent a smaller detachment. If they feared a riot, it well could have been the full cohort. Quite a military presence to arrest this preacher from Nazareth! Somehow Judas was the main man in the group because he would identify Jesus, and it says he received the group. He had told the officials that they would know who to arrest because he would kiss him. Judas did just that, and the betrayal was done.

The Earthly End of Judas

*Matthew 27:3-7 – Then when Judas, who had betrayed Him, saw that He had been condemned, he felt remorse and returned the thirty pieces of silver to the chief priests and elders, saying, "I have sinned by betraying innocent blood." But they said, "What is that to us? See to that yourself!" And he threw the pieces of silver into the temple sanctuary and departed; and he went away and **hanged himself**. The chief priests took the pieces of silver and said, "It is not lawful to put them into the temple treasury, since it is the price of blood." And they conferred together and with the money bought the Potter's Field as a burial place for strangers. For this reason that field has been called the Field of Blood to this day.*

*Acts 1:18-20 – (Now this man acquired a field with the price of his wickedness, and falling headlong, he **burst open in the middle and all his intestines gushed out**. And it became known to all who were living in Jerusalem; so that in their own language that field was called Hakeldama, that is, Field of Blood.)*

After seeing it all unfold, with the result that Jesus was condemned to die, Judas felt regret and remorse. He tried to assuage his guilt by returning the thirty pieces of silver to the chief priests, but they wouldn't take it back, so his burden of guilt was not lightened. We don't know how long he stayed alive, but it was long enough for the chief priests to buy the Field of Blood, where in desperation Judas went and hanged himself. Apparently his dead body stayed hanging quite some time. When it finally fell down, his body burst open and his guts gushed out. The Field of Blood became a place people viewed as cursed, and only "strangers" were buried there.

The Spiritual End of Judas (Destiny)

In John 17:12 Jesus referred to Judas as the son of perdition. This is a telling statement from our Lord. Perdition literally means "one who is destined to be lost." In John 6:70 Jesus said that Judas was a devil. In Luke 22:3 it says that Satan entered into Judas and he then went to the chief priests to make the betrayal bargain for thirty pieces of silver. In Luke 22:22 Jesus said "woe to that man (Judas) by whom He (Jesus) is betrayed!" John 13:27 indicates that after Jesus had given the morsel to Satan, to identify him as the betrayer, Satan then entered into him. After Jesus had been arrested and was condemned to die, Judas felt regret at what he had done. He felt remorse, which is a combination of regret and sorrow, but not necessarily repentance. He told the chief priests that he had sinned by betraying innocent blood. But that is not repentance. Scripture tells us that God is not willing that any should perish, but that all should come to repentance. To repent actually means to stop doing the wrong thing and to begin doing the right thing. After expressing remorse and confessing sin, the next action that Judas took was to commit suicide.

Judas was not predestined by God to sin. We are given insights into his character: he stole from the shared money box, and was more concerned with money than honoring Jesus. He made a deal for money to betray the Lord. By choosing money over the Lord, he allowed Satan to enter into his heart. By moving forward to betray Jesus in the garden, he allowed Satan more control of his soul. Judas was not predestined by God, but his character and conduct created his own destiny: to be lost.

John's Final Night Reflections on Betrayal

John vividly remembered the moments when Peter directed him to ask the Lord who the betrayer was. Some of the disciples didn't hear or understand the "morsel" interaction between Judas and Jesus. But John was right there, up close. What a moment to witness. And he also remembered that special prayer that Jesus offered up to the Father on their behalf. Unity, preservation and protection was provided for them and for all who believed in Jesus through their testimony – except for Judas the betrayer, the son of perdition. He was destined to be lost.

Perhaps more importantly, John remembered the lesson Jesus taught by washing the disciples' feet. It was a lesson in how to humbly serve one another in the Body of Christ. There were two unique foot notes that he remembered. Firstly Jesus declared that His followers that serve one another in the way He had taught them were chosen by Him and His Father to receive special blessings (Jesus made it clear that Judas was not one that would receive these special blessings). As it says in Colossians 3:23, 24 – Whatever you do, do your work heartily, as for the Lord rather than for men, knowing that from the Lord you will receive the reward of the inheritance. It is the Lord Christ whom you serve. In John 13:18 Jesus did make it clear that Judas was not one that would receive these special blessings. Secondly Jesus made a point of emphasizing that Judas the betrayer was unclean. He had washed all of their feet, including Judas the unclean one, and used that as the example of humble service that they were to follow. It's easier for us to humbly serve other humble people. But we would rather avoid humbly serving the ones who are unclean betrayers. This is a reminder to all of us of how to serve: love your enemies, do good to those who hate you, pray for those who despitefully use you.

Chapter Ten

PETER, PETER, PETER

So strong...So weak...So human

We get the fullest glimpse of the life and character of one of the apostles, when we follow Peter, as he traveled with Jesus. One of the select twelve disciples, who were also called apostles, his human qualities, both weak and strong, make him a man we can identify with. He was the one who made the great proclamation about Jesus: "Thou are the Christ, the Son of the living God!" He was also the one who actually took Jesus to the side and rebuked Him for discussing His coming death in Jerusalem, and had Jesus respond to him, "Get thee behind me, Satan!" On that final night, when Jesus said that Peter would deny Him three times before the night was over, Peter loudly disagreed, declaring that he would never deny Jesus. When Jesus and His followers were in the garden, surrounded by Roman soldiers and officers from the chief priests, Peter impulsively swung his sword, cutting off a servant's ear. This was in the midst of hundreds of soldiers! Following that he did deny Jesus three times, actually swearing as he proclaimed that he did not know Him. He was an impulsive loudmouth; but was transformed by the resurrection of Jesus, the personal instruction he received from the Lord and the baptism of the Holy Spirit on the Day of

Pentecost. He became the great preacher and leader of the New Testament, now full of the Holy Spirit. What a man...what a human...what a Christian!

John records three of Peter's final night interactions. Let's see what John was remembering and emphasizing for us.

*John 13:6-11 – So He came to Simon Peter. He said to Him, "Lord, do you wash my feet?" Jesus answered and said to him, 'What I do you do not realize now, but you will understand hereafter. Peter said to Him, "**Never shall you wash my feet!**" Jesus answered him, "If I do not wash you, you have no part with Me." Simon Peter said to him, "Lord, then wash not only my feet, but also my hands and my head." Jesus said to him, "He who has bathed needs only to wash his feet, but is completely clean; and you are clean, but not all of you." For He knew the one who was betraying Him; for this reason he said, "Not all of you are clean."*

I think all of the apostles were quiet, embarrassed, convicted and ashamed as Jesus was washing their feet, one at a time. It was unnatural and very uncomfortable to have their Leader doing this. And so He came to Peter. It looks like he may have been the last one Jesus came to: number twelve. All of the others had maintained the uncomfortable silence while Jesus washed their feet, but not Peter. Incredulous at the whole scene, he stopped the Lord: "You're going to wash my feet?" Jesus tried to calm him: "This doesn't make sense to you right now, but after I explain it you'll understand." Peter just got more volatile and adamant: "No way am I going to allow you to wash my feet!" This was a confrontational scene. I can imagine the other apostles sitting there, with mouths fallen open, not knowing what was going to happen next. Peter was not thoughtfully considering what was going on. He was not reviewing the unique and profound ways that Jesus had taught them over the last 3 ½ years. He was not even being submissively respectful to his Lord. He was allowing his very strong feelings to burst forth and dictate his words. How would we say it: "Open mouth before engaging brain, and insert foot!" That's what Peter was doing. Christ had worked with this volatile, strong-willed, impulsive fisherman for three-plus years, and knew that He had to shock him into shutting his mouth, controlling his emotions, submitting his will and opening his mind to what the Lord was doing: "Peter, if I don't wash you, you're out!" That shut Peter up. Still, in a final effort to express his commitment to the Lord in his own impulsive way, Peter cried out: "Wash all of me, Lord; I'm with you all the way!"

Peter was a proud man, full of self-confidence. He had a high opinion of himself; his self worth was strong. That can be good; but combined with strong will and impulsive behavior, it often leads to foolishness. When the Lord is doing something, we should not get in the way. When the Lord is saying something, we should listen. If we get in the way, or we're not listening, the Lord is going to have to shut us down, for our own good. Have you ever had the Lord telling you to do something that you didn't want to do? I have. Has He ever prompted you to do something or say something, and you have argued with Him because you didn't understand, or just didn't want to do it? I have. What does that say about our own will, our own pride? Maybe we have a little bit of Peter in us?

John 13:22-24 – The disciples began looking at one another, at a loss to know of which one He was speaking. There was reclining on Jesus' bosom one of his disciples, whom Jesus loved. So Simon Peter gestured to him, and said to him, "Tell us who it is of whom He is speaking."

I want us to really see the picture of the final night. The things Jesus was saying, the actions He was taking were extraordinary and phenomenal. Yes, the apostles had seen many wonderful and phenomenal things in their time with Jesus. But this final night was packed with lessons, symbolism, concepts and teachings that were almost like an emergency survival course. Jesus was about to be taken from them and killed. It was bizarre! Jesus had just shared with them the Passover bread and wine: the first communion, with its symbolism of His crucifixion. It was a large room, so they were sitting around, perhaps in groups of two or three, talking among themselves, but not really hearing or paying attention to everything that was being said in the room. Suddenly Jesus says, "One of you is going to betray Me." Now what? Nobody said anything because nobody knew what to say. Nobody, except Peter. He took charge of the subtle investigation. He had been kind of loud and blustery, so he needed to use a little more caution and stealth, but still get what he wanted. "Psst! John! Tell us who He's talking about." John was the youngest apostle, and pretty much followed where Peter led. And as the youngest apostle he had a close, loving relationship with Jesus. At the moment he was closest to Him, almost leaning on his chest. He was the perfect one to get more information. So Peter set John into motion to get the information he needed. What does that tell us about Peter? We have already seen that his strong will and impulsiveness led at times to foolishness on his part. He had just been shut down. It was pretty close to being set in the corner and told to be quiet and learn. Yet his self confidence and leadership tendencies would not allow him to remain inactive when something needed to be checked out. But he held his impulsiveness and volatility in check this time. That was not an easy thing; he had been strong-willed and impulsive most of his life. But he managed to seize control of himself, and work through another person to achieve the goal. Good lesson for us: when our character weaknesses make it difficult to move forward and accomplish a task, with the

Lord's help, we can hold our weaknesses in check, and we can get help from the team around us, our fellow Christian brothers and sisters. As a matter of fact that's why God calls us the body of Christ. Each and every one of us is a member of the body, but one member can't do it all. Yet with our fellow members, we can accomplish the task, whether it's through subtle or overt actions.

*John 13:36-38 – Simon Peter said to Him, "Lord, where are You going?" Jesus answered, "Where I go you cannot follow Me now; but you will follow later." Peter said to him, "Lord, why can I not follow you right now? **I will lay down my life for you.**" Jesus answered, "Will you lay down your life for Me? Truly, truly, I say to you, a rooster will not crow until you deny Me three times."*

"So, Lord, where are You going?"

Parts of this final night conversation between Jesus and Peter are recorded in all of the four gospels. Those records show the full spectrum of emotions and character on the parts of Peter and Jesus. Right now I just want to focus on what John was remembering and recording for us. Remember, he had probably read all three of the other gospels, so there was a reason that he wrote what he did, inspired by the Holy Spirit. Jesus told them, "Where I am going, you cannot come." He was referring to His temporary separation from His disciples. He was to be arrested, tried, crucified, buried and resurrected. He knew He would be conquering death, hell and the grave, and His disciples would not be coming with Him into that. So He told them that. But Peter — being Peter — wouldn't accept that. He started to set up his argument. If Jesus would give

91

him the details of where He was going, then Peter would be able to construct his argument as to why he could come with Him. "So, Lord, where are You going?" Jesus knew what Peter was trying to do, so He gave Peter the opportunity to back down gently. "You can't follow Me now, but you will get the chance to follow me later." Peter's strategy of logical persuasion wasn't working out, so being the impulsive "mouth first, brain later" disciple, he let loose: "Why can't I come now? I would die for you!" Then Jesus shut him down. "You're going to deny Me three times before the night is over." This was such a shock for Peter. We know his emotions were in turmoil, and his pride was definitely taking a hit. John doesn't tell us, but the other gospels indicate that Peter still kept talking: "I will never deny you!" Peter was a long way from understanding that what Jesus says is always right, and it doesn't pay to argue the point with Him. Now how often has that happened to us? If Jesus says something that we're not sure of, or don't agree with, we want to "discuss" it. (That's our nice word for arguing). It's a funny thing, but most of the time we do almost all the talking and God does almost all the listening. Man, is that backwards! It took Peter years to learn the lesson: Don't argue with God; just listen and do it. Father knows best.

From John's remembrances of Peter on that final night we are presented with issues of the soul.

Emotions. Peter was full of zeal. That literally means to burn hot. His loud, blustery volatility and impulsiveness stemmed from strong emotions, and especially from strong emotions winning out and controlling his actions.

Intellect. Peter was full of pride and self-confidence. Pride is assigned to our intellect because it is our opinion of self, and that is a position of thought and intellect. Pride of self, when balanced with humility can be very positive to our leadership skills. But if your pride of self is not balanced, it can lead to thoughts of superiority and a manner of arrogance that challenges the leadership over us. Or it can lead to a dominating, "lording it over" approach. We become the first to speak and the first to take charge. As James 1:19 tells us — everyone must be quick to hear, slow to speak and slow to anger.

Volition (will). God wants every one of us to be strong willed. To be strong willed and fervent for the right things is the kind of volition God wants us to have. But if our emotional weaknesses tip us over into self will, then it all turns bad. Beyond fervent, we become adamant in our own positions; argumentative and confrontational.

Our pattern of communication with Jesus is often not good, because we spend almost the whole time talking, and very little time listening. The next time you have a conversation with Him, see how much you talk and how much you listen. Peter needed to learn to be silent and listen to what Jesus was saying. We need to keep our emotions under control, balanced by our intellect and will, and tempered by His Holy Spirit. Zeal and fervency can be a good thing.

Zeal + Fervency + Pride only in self = Self deception and a fall. Result: Foolishness

Zeal + Fervency + Pride balanced by humility = Self Identity and promotion. Result: Wisdom

Chapter Eleven

GLORY, GLORY, GLORY!

Light...Bright...Dazzling...The Cross

John 13:31, 32 – Therefore when He had gone out, Jesus said, "Now is the Son of Man glorified, and God is glorified in Him; if God is glorified in Him, God will also glorify Him in Himself, and will glorify Him immediately.

John 16:14 – He (the Spirit of truth) *will glorify Me, for He will take of Mine and will disclose it to you.*

John 17:1-5 – Jesus spoke these things: and lifting up His eyes to heaven, He said, "Father, the hour has come; glorify Your Son, that the Son may glorify You, even as You gave Him authority over all flesh, that to all whom You have given Him, He may give eternal life. This is eternal life, that they may know You, the only true God, and Jesus Christ whom You have sent. I glorified You on the earth, having accomplished the work which You have given Me to do. Now, Father, glorify Me together with Yourself, with the glory which I had with You before the world was.

Glory, glorify, glorified. These words are used a lot in Scripture, and we hear them in our churches regularly. The songs that we sing often speak of the glory of God. But the words seem to have a vague cloud of meaning that we really are uncertain of. We know God has it, or should be acknowledged with it, but it still remains an unclear concept.

As my children were growing up, we were all very involved with 4H. We believed the children learned great lessons of management and responsibility with their animals and projects. It all culminated in the county and state fairs. I used to say that the 4H rewards were a great combination of glory and honor for the kids. The many ribbons, certificates and trophies they received each year were the "honor." The premium-points money they received was the glory. They loved getting that premium check and spending it on whatever they wanted. Glorious! Even though I was the one using the word, that really wasn't what glory means.

The Greek word (doxa) carries a very physical meaning: brightness, splendor, radiance, glory, majesty, sublimity. It has been used to describe the burning brightness of the sun. It could refer to the manner in which someone was clothed: adorned with lustre.

When an angel of the Lord appeared to the shepherds caring for their flocks, to announce the birth of Christ in Bethlehem, it indicates that the angel suddenly appeared, and the glory of the Lord shone around them, and they were terribly frightened. Something about the appearance of the angel scared them to death! Maybe brightness, shining, awesome angel presence; the glory shined, so it must have been bright.

In a number of secular Greek references the word was used with regard to magic. When a particular point of revelation occurred in whatever magical process or presentation was occurring, glory was seen or appeared. This may have been some gimmick to awe the audience or client, and it was something bright and visual. Modern day magicians often use big poofs of smoke and flashing lights to indicate something "magical" is happening. Nowadays we "sophisticated" observers know it is just a show, but back in the first century people often thought it was showing some kind of spirit or divine presence. That brings us to a deeper meaning that developed in the Jewish community.

The Jewish people over hundreds of years had developed an awe of the glory of God. It started with the tabernacle that they had constructed in the wilderness, during the time of Moses. When it had been built, the presence of the LORD came to dwell in the holy of holies, and the cloudiness or brightness was so overpowering that Moses couldn't even stay in the area. This has been referred to as the shekinah glory of God, and it carried the definite concept of the presence of God; God was dwelling there. It was definitely something that they saw with their physical eyes. In John 1:14 in referring to Jesus Christ coming in the flesh, it says the Word became flesh and dwelled among them, and they saw the glory of the only begotten from the Father. Literally it says they "beheld his glory," and that meant seeing with their physical eyes. The very presence of God the Son in the flesh was equated with the shekinah glory of God.

It encompasses the dwelling place, the very presence of God.

In reference to God, glory refers to the bright appearance and more. It encompasses the dwelling place, the very presence of God. Jesus Christ in the flesh was and is the glory of God. And it represented still more than that. The incarnation of God was for one purpose: the salvation of mankind through

His blood shed on the cross. The cross of Jesus Christ is the glory of God.

The six key points in these Scriptures are as follows:

1. The atoning work of the cross glorified Christ.

2. The Father glorified the Son.

3. Christ glorified the Father.

4. The Holy Spirit brings glory to the Son.

5. When Christ was glorified, it also glorified the Father.

6. The glorifying is with the glory that the Godhead had before the beginning.

Boiling the six ideas down, we can analyze them in three categories:

The atoning work of the cross glorified Christ. When Jesus said the hour has come, and called upon the Father to glorify Him, He was referring to His arrest, crucifixion and resurrection. This was the focal point of the Word becoming flesh and dwelling among us. He emptied Himself of His divine powers and took the form of a bond-servant. He was made in the likeness of men, and being found in appearance as a man, He humbled Himself to the point of death; His death on the cross was the culmination of the incarnation. It was the reason He became flesh and dwelt among us. The event of the cross was in and of itself the glorification of Christ, so He could say, "Now is the Son of Man glorified."

Glory throughout the Godhead. Christ commanded the Father to glorify Him. The Son being glorified also glorified the Father. We see the Father glorifying the Son because of the cross. We see that the Son glorified the Father by being on the earth, and dying on the cross. We also see that the Holy Spirit glorifies the Son by disclosing to all of us the divine glory of the cross. We know that the fullness of the Godhead dwells in the Son in bodily form. God died on the cross for us. Christ dying on the cross is the physical manifestation of God's glory that we got to see with our physical eyes. The glory of God is the glory of the cross.

Glory from before the world began. Whoa! I can understand the concept of glory that is light, bright and dazzling. I'm trying to wrap my mind around the glory of God manifested so that I can see it with my physical eyes. I'm beginning to appreciate the glory that is the cross of Christ. But before the world was created, before humans were created and fell into sin, before the plan of salvation was accomplished through the cross of Jesus Christ, before all that, God had glory. I know God has always existed, but I haven't given any thought to what God was like before creation. The glory God had before there was light; the glory God had before His manifested presence was needed by humans; the glory God had before we needed to see it with our physical eyes; that glory of God was the glory used to glorify Christ at the cross. I can't picture what God's pre-creation glory was like. It had to be beyond anything we could think. That is how glorious the cross of Jesus Christ is!

The more I learn about the glory of God, the more I realize that I cannot conceive it. But I can appreciate the glory of God in the cross of Christ, and I am humbled by it, and so thankful for it. To God be the glory.

Chapter Twelve

PEACE AND TRIBULATION

Tribulation is possible, but God's peace is certain!

The classic joke about beauty pageant contestants concerns their answer to the question of what they want or wish for. The answer: "world peace." Remember the chorus from that famous Beatles song? "All we are saying is give peace a chance." We humans seem to express again and again that we want peace. And yet we can't seem to accomplish it.

Some famous peace quotes:

"If someone thinks that love and peace is
a cliché that must have been left behind
in the Sixties, that's his problem.
Love and peace are eternal"
—John Lennon

"Peace cannot be kept by force,
it can only be achieved by understanding"
—Albert Einstein

"But peace does not rest in the charters and covenants alone. It lies in the hearts and minds of all people. So let us not rest all our hopes on parchment and on paper, let us strive to build peace, a desire for peace, a willingness to work for peace in the hearts and minds of all of our people. I believe that we can. I believe the problems of human destiny are not beyond the reach of human beings."
— John F. Kennedy

"The true and solid peace of nations consists not in equality of arms, but in mutual trust alone."
— Pope John XXIII

"If you want peace, work for justice."
— Pope Paul VI

"To reach peace, teach peace."
— Pope John Paul II

I reviewed a lot of famous peace quotes from internet sites that emphasize the need and desire for peace among men. In one way or another, the quotes all encouraged men to aspire to the bringing of peace, and that through their efforts peace will come. The problem is a simple one: without Christ man is not able or willing to achieve peace. Those who seemed to cry the loudest for peace also were the ones who opposed Christianity, and believed that religion was an obstacle to peace. The truth: without the Lord Jesus Christ, the hearts of men will never come to peace.

Through the ages humanity has for the most part been content with a negative definition of peace: peace is the absence of war, or the opposite of war. But within the Jewish community, through the ages, peace has meant much more than that. It is a positive state of harmony. It has had a distinctly messianic framework; they believed that part of the messianic salvation would be a state of peace. Jesus, as Christ, the son of the living God, had a unique position of peace, and freely passed that on to His disciples. On the final night, Jesus wanted them to know that persecution would come to them, and that they might also face degrees of tribulation, but they would overcome that because of His peace.

John 14:27 – Peace I leave with you; My peace I give to you; not as the world gives do I give to you. Do not let your heart be troubled, nor let it be fearful.

John 16:31-33 – Jesus answered them, "Do you now believe? Behold, an hour is coming, and has already come, for you to be scattered, each to his own home, and to leave Me alone; and yet I am not alone, because the Father is with Me. These things I have spoken to you, so that in Me you may have peace. In the world you have tribulation, but take courage; I have overcome the world.

Tribulation

The Greek word for tribulation (thlipsis) can mean oppression, affliction, distress, anguish. It has a base meaning of being pressed or under pressure. In some first century harbors, there were narrow straits that entered into the harbor bay. If the entry straits were narrower than usual, and required added navigational challenge, they were said to have tribulation. The word has a very broad strength of application, all the way from an annoyance to the point of death. So at the mild end of the scale, having someone irritate you could be referred to as tribulation; and at the severe end of the scale, the same Greek word is used in Revelation to refer to the Great Tribulation of the end times.

When I was a high school teenager, I remember one day going out to the local lake with my friend, instead of getting to school on time. I knew we would be in trouble when we got to school two hours late. Back in that day being that late was referred to as "skipping classes," and could get detention time or suspension from school. With my friend, I concocted an excuse. We took the spare out of the trunk and changed it with a good tire. Then we let the air out of the good tire, and threw it into the trunk. When we drove into the parking lot at school, the vice principal, Mr. Cooper, met us with clear threats of writing us up. I told my lies, and opened the trunk to show the flat tire. He grudgingly accepted the excuse, and I got through my tribulation.

Another time just three years later, I was a combat medic, caught in an ambush with several wounded men, and only escaped that tribulation by the aggressive action of U.S. Cobra gunships passing over and firing their mini-guns at the enemy to get us free. You can see that tribulation can be mild or severe. On this final night Jesus knew that light and heavy tribulation could be coming to His followers, and He wanted them to come through both kinds with victory. From the world, they might have tribulation come their way, but they absolutely had His peace with them and in them to bring them through. Jesus overcame the world, so with Him in them, and they in Him, they would overcome the world. Take courage!

Reaction to Tribulation

Troubled hearts. Jesus did not want His followers to have troubled hearts because of the tribulation they might experience from the world. The Greek word for troubled (tarasso) was pretty strong; meaning to be disturbed or unsettled; to be thrown into confusion; to be affected by grief and/or anxiety. It has a base meaning of being shaken together or stirred up. I grew up in the Northwest, and remember, as a child, going out into the yard to play after there had been a heavy rain. I loved playing in puddles; not just stomping through them, but getting down carefully by them to see what I could see. If I was careful the water was clear, and I could see different bugs, worms and plants trying to get back to normal life without being under water. It was amazing what I could see. But at the end of my observations, I loved using a stick to stir up the puddle. It would get so murky and muddy that I couldn't see anything, and I was sure that the bugs couldn't either! I was "troubling" the water so much that no one/nothing could see what was happening or what to do. That kind of troubling can happen to Christians; we may be the cause or others may be the cause. Depending upon how serious the circumstances are, it can be troubling, frightening or even terrifying. Jesus did not want that for His followers. So He commanded: don't be troubled!

John 14:1 – Do not let your heart be troubled; believe in God, believe also in Me.

He used the same Greek word earlier that evening. Jesus had communicated to them that He was going away (in the arrest, trial and crucifixion) and they could not come with Him, but once He was back (resurrected), they would follow Him; and He wanted them to follow Him in loving one another. Peter had taken issue with this, declaring that he would follow Jesus, no matter how hard it got. Jesus had to set him back in his place, so He prophesied that Peter would deny Him three times that very night. All of this put the disciples in an uneasy and unsettled mood, so Jesus had to remind them that they could avoid having troubled hearts by strongly believing in Him.

> It just kicks in the "flee" action,
> out of extreme fear or cowardice.

Fearful hearts. Neither did Jesus want His followers to have fearful hearts because of tribulation from the world. The Greek word for fearful (deiliao) is used only here in the New Testament and has the meaning of being cowardly because of overwhelming, intimidating fear. The word was used in a secular document of the time; it was a communication from a condemned man to the emperor of Rome; the prisoner lamented that he might break down in cowardly fear at the moment of execution. The word could be used of the fearful feeling one would get if a wild beast suddenly appeared. But it carried more meaning than just the sudden rush of adrenalin. People often talk about the "fight or flight" dilemma. In any given situation of danger, it is best if reasoning kicks in long enough to figure out if it's wiser to fight or flee. But the kind of fear in this Greek word doesn't allow for reasoning or wisdom: it just kicks in the "flee" action, out of extreme fear or cowardice. Jesus did not want His disciples to be overwhelmed in this fearful way by tribulation from the world.

To paraphrase His words: "I command you to keep control of your heart. Don't allow such strong troubling that everything gets muddy and murky, and you can't see! Don't allow an overwhelming fear to drive you into cowardly flight. You're My followers. Man up!

Peace

This word for peace refers to the opposite of armed conflict or war. As I mentioned earlier, it is not just the absence of war or conflict, but the total opposite of it: a state of positive harmony.

Jesus leaves peace. This Greek word (aphiami) for "leave" is definitely talking about a separation, and it can have a negative or a positive context. Back in the first century they had the same kind of marital problems that we have these days. Sometimes the marriage ended with a divorce. This Greek word for "leave" was used in a legal sense of divorce when the man left the woman. That's a negative use of the word.

John 16:32 – Behold an hour is coming, and has already come, for you to be scattered, each to his own home, and to leave Me alone; and yet I am not alone, because the Father is with Me.

John 14:18 – I will not leave you as orphans; I will come to you.

Jesus used the word in a negative way when He referred to the disciples abandoning Him in the next twenty-four hours, and leaving Him alone. He also used it in the negative way of leaving someone as orphans, although His statement was absolutely positive because He was coming back and they would <u>not</u> be left as orphans.

But the word was also used for something positive being left. My wife has done a great job of having wills made out for us, in the event of our death. As I was reading over the two wills, I did notice that her will had many specifics in it, regarding several personal possessions. I didn't put any of that in my will; I was more general in divisions and percentages. But she wanted to make sure that certain items went to her daughters and her grandchildren; items of jewelry and family heirlooms. (Sounds like a classic difference between men and women, huh?) Back in the first century, just like now, when a person died, and left a will that bequeathed certain gifts or properties to their friends or relatives, they were said to be "leaving" something for someone. This is a very positive use of the word. When Jesus said "peace I leave with you," it was like a bequest; a very positive one!

Jesus gives His peace. Give (Greek – didomi) is a very clear word meaning to give; to grant; to bestow. This form of giving is not earned or worked for. 100% of the giving is done by the giver; 0% of the giving is done by the recipient. That is the clear meaning of this very straight forward term. But humans can take the clearest of concepts and twist it to their own ends.

In our retirement years, my wife and I have purchased a 40' motor home to travel in and see the sites. It's like owning your very own beach cottage; only you can take this one anywhere you want to travel. I love driving it, and we have had some incredible trips with our grand kids. It does cost to stay in the RV parks, so we don't travel as often as I would like to. About a month ago I got a post card in the mail that offered three nights and four days in a great RV park at no cost. It was a free gift! Then I noticed that we would be required to attend a 90-minute sales presentation on membership in a national RV park organization. ????? I looked over the community where the RV park was located, and realized it could be a really great mini-trip with our granddaughters. Texas dinosaur country! But as I discussed it with my wife, that 90-minute sales presentation caused both of us concern. Several years ago, we had traveled to a vacation resort and had to sit through a "90-minute" sales presentation that lasted almost five hours. Although I said "no thank you" a number of times, they kept passing us off to higher level managers, and pressing, pressing, pressing. I had to get very loud and very angry before they would give up on the sale! So back to the RV trip.

Even though the RV trip offer was a free gift, we decided that dealing with another sales presentation would cost us too much. My point is this: it's not really a gift if there are strings attached. That's what humans can do to the concept of giving.

But Jesus does not give as the world gives. To benefit from His peace, there's no extra effort, no special works, no "sales pitch cost" that will come our way. Jesus gave to His disciples the Messianic peace that only He could give; His perfect peace and harmony that lasts forever. And that is what He gives to us also.

In Jesus His disciples would have peace. He said they might get tribulation from the world, but it wouldn't matter because in Jesus they would absolutely have peace!

Reaction to Peace

Take courage. Giving this kind of permanent Messianic peace and harmony, Jesus rallied the troops. The word means to take courage; cheer up; be of good cheer. It's the idea of being infused with a truth that turns your feelings around. I will be the first one to tell you that I am a foodie, when it comes to my emotions. If I am under stress, or feeling down or defeated, it's amazing how certain foods can turn my moods around. My wife's apple pie with vanilla ice cream; her freshly baked chocolate chip cookies; hot, buttered cinnamon rolls from the local Whataburger; my wife's moist cheese cake, topped with cherries (that she only fixes for me once a year on my birthday); red velvet cake with thick butter cream frosting; pecan pie baked just right; pumpkin pie piled high with Kool Whip; hello dolly 7-layer cookies; chocolate fudge; pecan coconut German chocolate cake pie; maybe I'm not a foodie; maybe I'm a "dessertic!' (I just heard on the end of year TV reviews that they are removing the word "foodie" from the dictionary….it's just too cliché). Any of these desserts make me happy pretty quickly. But my happy doesn't last all that long, and the stress or downer feelings return.

Jesus offered the permanent solution to His disciples. No matter what the world threw at them, they didn't need to allow it to get them down. If they infused their soul with His truth, they could take courage and move forward. What truth: that Jesus has overcome the world. This Greek word for overcome had a legal sense of winning the case. When Jesus overcame the world, He won the case!

In the world we may have tribulation. In Jesus we absolutely have His peace. The tribulation may, or may not come. His peace absolutely will be there.

Shall we say that tribulation is part of life for the Christian in the world? Or shall we say that because we have peace in Jesus, and He has overcome the world, we don't need to lie down and accept that tribulation is ours to experience? We can take courage from His peace and be overcomers with Him. Which shall we choose? Do you want to win the case?

Chapter Thirteen

WHY'S EVERYBODY ALWAYS PICKIN' ON ME?

Persecution will come...How will we respond?

In many parts of the world today, real and dangerous persecution of Christians is happening. One could say that we have it pretty easy in the United States, when compared to the first century church or other parts of our twenty-first century world. Just take a look at what can be found reported on the internet:

PAKISTAN: CHRISTIAN PROFESSOR ARRESTED FOR BLASPHEMY

A Christian professor in Pakistan has been arrested for blasphemy after writing what were considered blasphemous comments in his blog. Qaiser Ayub, 40, has now been charged with insulting the prophet Mohammad, the same charge that leveled against Asia Bibi. The Christian Post reports that Ayub wrote the comments in his blog in 2011 and had been on the run from authorities for nearly three years. Ayub is now being held in a police station in Talagang; he was recently discovered teaching at a Labore school. The professor of computer science is represented by the advocacy group Legal Evangelical Association Development. Sardar Mushtaq Gill, Legal Evangelical Association Development's national director said that Ayub needs prayer. Gill continued, "The government must take immediate bold steps to repeal the blasphemy laws. The government has absolutely failed to protect its citizens' right to life and property. Christians in Pakistan are not safe as long as the current blasphemy laws exist. They are just misused to persecute them."

Carrie Dedrick | Editor, ChristianHeadlines.com | Tuesday, November 18, 2014

MURDER OF CHRISTIAN COUPLE BRINGS PAKISTAN'S BLASPHEMY LAWS INTERNATIONAL ATTENTION

Pakistan's blasphemy laws are coming under fire around the world. The criticism comes just after Christian couple Shama and Shahzad Masih were murdered because of a blasphemy accusation against the couple. "This incident has not just exposed Pakistan's treatment of its non-Muslim citizens, but also the prevailing hatred against them," Nasir Saeed wrote in a column for Christianity Today. "Extremism and hate of religious minorities, especially Christians, has permeated Pakistani society and is devouring it from the inside." Saeed writes that if the government had better handled punishing extremists of previous crimes then the killing of the Masihs could have been avoided. "Mere statements of condemnation won't work anymore," Saeed said. "In today's world where religion is considered a personal matter and a basic human right, and religious freedom is protected and guaranteed, such atrocious acts of killing in the name of religion are beyond imagination in a civilized world, and yet they regularly happen to Christians," he added. In the column, Saeed asked that Prime Minister Nawaz Sharif work to change the blasphemy law after attempts by General Musharraf and Benazir Bhutto to change the law failed.

Amanda Casanova | Religion Today Contributing Writer | Monday, November 17, 2014

DAUGHTER OF IMPRISONED CHINESE PASTOR DETAINED BY AUTHORITIES

Zhang Shanshan, the daughter of imprisoned pastor Zhang Shaojie, has reportedly been detained by Chinese authorities; it is believed that Zhang Shanshan is being held in a hotel against her will. Pastor Zhang was arrested in November 2013 for allegedly gathering a crowd which disrupted public order and committing fraud. He was sentenced to 12 years in prison in July at a trial that was not announced to his lawyers; American officials have called for his release. Zhang's daughter was reportedly taken into custody on Wednesday (Nov. 5) by unidentified men. A text that Zhang Shanshan sent her husband Hua CheeChuan read, "Nonle Hotel, help me!" Hua believes Zhang shanshan was detained to prevent her from speaking about her father's wrongful imprisonment. "They try to cover up the ugly things in the country, and they don't want the outside world to know what is going on in China," he said. "So I think that's why they've arrested them, and put them somewhere else."

Carrie Dedrick | Editor, ChristianHeadlines.com | Thursday, November 06, 2014

CHRISTIANS JAILED FOR RIOTING, AFTER BEING PERSONALLY ATTACKED AND HAVING TWO HOMES DAMAGED

Four Christians in Maharashtra state, one 70 years old, were released on bail today after more than two weeks in jail, accused of "rioting" when Hindu extremists attacked them and damaged two of their homes. The incident in Kamseth village, Nasik District in western India began on Oct. 28 when the Hindu extremists told Christians to remit 300 rupees (US$5) for the celebration of the Hindu festival of lights, or Diwali. The Christians submitted half the amount, which the Hindus later angrily returned to them, area church leader Prem Barnabas told Morning Star News. The Hindus summoned four Christians from two families – 70-year-old Govind Janu Galat, Gulab Govind Galat, Dilip Laxu Galat and Sakaram Govind Galat – to the village's Hindu temple and told them to return the rest of the money so that they could use it to buy alcohol, reported the Evangelical Fellowship of India (EFI). The Christians readily gave the money back to them, but the extremists began pushing, beating and kicking them as they insulted their Christian faith, according to EFI. "Somehow three Christians managed to run away after a while, but the one who remained, Dilip Laxu Galat, was severely beaten up," Barnabas said. The assailants then hurled stones at the house of Govind Janu Galat and stole items and 10,000 rupees ($US163) from his home. The long-time Christian says he came to Christ 30 years ago after visiting a church service in which his sight was restored after a pastor prayed for him. They also stoned another house of one of the Christians, breaking wall tiles and half of the roof, and damaged the small shop of another. Fearing for their lives, the four Christians fled, hid in mountainous terrain, and called the police. Officers reached the site later that evening. Under cover of darkness, the Hindu mob pelted police with stones, breaking their vehicle windows, and roughed them up. The Christians had come out of their hiding place when the police arrived, and the Hindu extremists resumed their attack on them, a Harsul police official identified only as Kirtekar told Morning Star News. "The mob wanted to continue beating the Christians, and as a safety measure we took them inside our vehicle, which further agitated the attackers, and they started to stone our vehicles," he said. On the basis of the complaint filed by the attackers, however, police arrested the four Christians under accusations of "rioting," though the police official said they were arrested in order to "protect" them. Police also filed a First Information Report against the 14 assailants. "We managed to nab eight of them, and we also hope to arrest the others who have absconded," he said. On Nov. 1 the Hindu extremists again stoned the houses of the two Christians, and several Christians, including women and children, fled into the mountains in fear. They have since returned to their homes. "All our people are poor, and we wanted to have a compromise with the villagers," Barnabas said. "We have talked to the village head, and he is ready to help us in securing a compromise." Tension remains, however, and an agreement that would bring peace remained elusive. The seed of conflict and hatred in Kamseth village appears to have been planted by the area leader of the Hindu extremist World Hindu Council (VHP), Promod Kurkani, according to the church leaders. He was once banned from a neighboring village, Ether, for spreading hateful propaganda against Christians, they said. "Ether village is a strong Christian community," Barnabas said. "After the village leaders realized that he had been trying to fill the minds of the simple villagers with his hate agendas, they banned him from staying there one year ago." Relatives had fasted and prayed for the four Christians while they were jailed. "Their faith in the Lord is exemplary and very touching," Barnabas said.

Courtesy: Morning Star News
Publication date: November 14, 2014

Pakistan, India, China: Arrested for putting Christian comments on your blog; murdered for blasphemy accusation; attacked and beaten, then arrested for "rioting;" your homes attacked and damaged; driven into the mountains to avoid being attacked; detained because your father, a Christian pastor, is imprisoned; these are a few of the things reported in November 2014. Maybe we Christians in America have it easier than we think. There are times that people look down on us, criticize us or treat us with contempt simply because we profess our relationship with Jesus Christ. That can be difficult because we want everybody to like us. There are also times that we Christians conduct ourselves in an offensive or unwise manner, and receive opposition as a result. When we bring contempt or opposition upon ourselves through our own failure to present the love of Christ, that's our bad, and we deserve what we get.

From my adolescent years I remember a song by the Coasters: "Charlie Brown."

Fe-fe, fi-fi, fo-fo, fum
I smell smoke in the auditorium

Charlie Brown, Charlie Brown
He's a clown, that Charlie Brown
He's gonna get caught
Just you wait and see
(Why's everybody always pickin' on me)

That's him on his knees
I know that's him

Yeah, from 7 come 11
Down in the boys' gym

Charlie Brown, Charlie Brown
He's a clown, that Charlie Brown
He's gonna get caught
Just you wait and see
(Why's everybody always pickin' on me)

Who's always writing on the wall
Who's always goofing in the hall
Who's always throwing spit balls
Guess who (who, me) yeah, you

Who walks in the classroom, cool and slow
Who calls the English teacher, Daddy-O

Charlie Brown, Charlie Brown
He's a clown, that Charlie Brown
He's gonna get caught
Just you wait and see
(Why's everybody always pickin' on me)

That's not persecution; that's just poor judgment.

The whole song was a joke, pointing out half-a-dozen things Charlie Brown did wrong; he pretty much did everything wrong, but didn't think that anyone should hold him responsible for the stupid or thoughtless things he was doing. "Why's everybody always pickin' on me?" I bring this up to make a point: sometimes Christians are goofing off, or doing crazy things or offensive things, and people react to them.

And the poor Christian feels persecuted: "Why's everybody always pickin' on me?" That's not persecution; that's just poor judgment.

I have just bounced you from the dangerous to the ridiculous in terms of persecution. Jesus knew that Christians through the ages would be persecuted. So on that final night he lined out the reasons, the hopes and the successful ways of handling persecution.

John 15:18-25 – If the world hates you, you know that it has hated Me before it hated you. If you were of the world, the world would love its own; but because you are not of the world, but I chose you out of the world, because of this the world hates you. Remember the word that I said to you, 'A slave is not greater than his master.' **If they persecuted Me, they will also persecute you;** *if they kept My word, they will keep yours also. But all these things they will do to you for My name's sake, because they do not know the One who sent Me. If I had not come and spoken to them, they would not have sin, but now they have no excuse for their sin. He who hates Me hates My Father also. If I had not done among them the works which no one else did, they would not have sin; but now they have both seen and hated Me and My Father as well. But they have done this to fulfill the word that is written in the Law, 'They hated Me without a cause.'*

Jesus helps us understand "the world." The world He is referring to encompasses the group of people that reject Him. He presented His word, a new truth that was not of the world they wanted. And He performed works, signs and wonders that no one else did, as a witness that He was the truth. In these verses He makes it clear that those who rejected Him go far beyond rejection into hate. They hated Him and took action to persecute Him. And He wanted His disciples to understand that the world would also hate and persecute them. What they were about to see happen to Him would also happen to them. But...they had seen Him and witnessed His works, signs and wonders, and chosen to keep His word. And it was worth it! He had chosen them, and any persecution was worth being His chosen disciples.

John 16:1-4 – These things I have spoken to you so that you may be kept from stumbling. They will make you outcasts from the synagogue, but an hour is coming for everyone who kills you to think that he is offering service to God. These things they will do because they have not known the Father or Me. But these things I have spoken to you, so that when their hour comes, you may remember that I told you of them. These things I did not say to you at the beginning, because I was with you.

Jesus knew that He was going to be separated from His disciples for a few days, by arrest, death and burial, and that would shake them to the core. He also knew that after the Day of Pentecost He would be with them, but in a different way: not physically with them, but spiritually with them, inside of them. He wanted them to be able to handle that without stumbling. The Greek word translated as stumbling– skandalidzoo – means to have a stumbling block or impediment put in the way; to be caused to stumble; to be caused to begin to mistrust and desert one whom you ought to trust in and obey; to be caused to fall away. Just as He had been made an outcast from the synagogues, and His opponents would believe they were serving God by killing Him, so the same would happen to His followers. Being ostracized from the only religious organization that they had known, and also being persecuted to the point of death could be overwhelming. Whether it was in the first century or it is the present day world, that kind of isolation and persecution could result in Christians turning back from the Lord, or doubting Him. The people who come against Christians do not know the Father or the Son. So the Lord communicated clearly to His disciples that He and the Father were one and that the Holy Spirit would come to them and testify of Jesus. He forewarned them of the coming rejection, persecution, and even death; but He also pointed them to the truth and the strength that would see them through the difficult times. Get in close, personal contact with the Holy Spirit inside of you, and He will give you witness of the truth: that God in His fullness is inside of you and will empower you to stand firm in the truth of the gospel. You need never stumble, being indwelled by the eternal, spiritual Word of God.

John 17:13-19 – But now I come to You; and these things I speak in the world so that they may have My joy made full in themselves. I have given them Your word; and the world has hated them, because they are not of the world, even as I am not of the world. I do not ask You to take them out of the world, but to keep them from the evil one. They are not of the world, even as I am not of the world. Sanctify them in the truth; Your word is truth. As You sent Me into the world, I also have sent them into the world. For their sakes I sanctify Myself, that they themselves also may be sanctified in truth.

That final night Jesus wanted His disciples to understand and embrace what they needed in order to go forth. He was the Word, and had given them the word of the Father. That word was the truth of the gospel in all its glory, and His word and His truth made them holy, that is, it made them a separated, consecrated, dedicated people for God's own possession. Being that, they were not of the world, and the world would hate them because of it.

And so He forewarned them of the hate and rejection, and even death that would come their way. He wanted them to face it all: eyes wide open with forewarning and understanding. Jesus had given them the witness of His word and truth, and they had embraced it. So He had chosen them, and they would be His successful witnesses! They would not be scandalized by the hatred and separation, because they would be tapped into God within them. The Holy Spirit would bear witness of Jesus, bringing everything He had said to their remembrance, and that would contribute to their successful witness. How does a Christian overcome persecution? By holding ever firmer to the truth that Jesus has given us...by embracing the Spirit of Truth within us, allowing Him to bring boldness to our declaration of the truth, and by practicing our separation from the world and our consecration to the truth of God. That "truth" path is the only path for us! Jesus brought us the witness of the Father's truth; the Holy Spirit witnesses to the very truth and words of Jesus, and we go forth to boldly testify and bear witness of the truth. In Christian tradition through the ages, when a Christian was killed he was referred to as a martyr. That came from the Greek word – martyria. The word is properly translated "to bear witness." Instead of focusing on the pain and death of persecution, we are to focus on bearing witness to the truth of the gospel of Jesus Christ. That people are saved by receiving the gospel of the cross of Christ is the all encompassing and overcoming truth of God. When we bear witness to the gospel truth with love and wisdom, any persecution that comes our way is of no importance.

Chapter Fourteen

FRUIT OF THE VINE

Abiding in the Vine

*John 15:1-11 – I am the true vine, and My Father is the vinedresser. Every branch in Me that does not bear fruit, He **takes away;** and every branch that bears fruit, He **prunes** it so that it may bear more fruit. You are already clean because of the word which I have spoken to you. Abide in Me, and I in you. As the branch cannot bear fruit of itself unless it abides in the vine, so neither can you unless you abide in Me. I am the vine, you are the branches; he who abides in Me and I in him, he bears much fruit, for apart from Me you can do nothing. If anyone does not abide in Me, he is **thrown away** as a branch and dries up; and they gather them, and **cast them into the fire** and they are burned. If you abide in Me, and My words abide in you, ask whatever you wish, and it will be done for you. My Father is glorified by this, that you bear much fruit, and so prove to be My disciples. Just as the Father has loved Me, I have also loved you; abide in My love. If you keep My commandments, you will abide in My love; just as I have kept My Father's commandments and abide in His love. These things I have spoken to you so that My joy may be in you, and that your joy may be made full.*

In the 1970's we had a lot of singing going on in the church that was very enjoyable, but maybe not as Biblical as we thought. I can remember sitting around a camp fire on the beach at night with a large group of young people and a couple of guitars, just singing our lungs out. It was great! We were Jesus people, and the world was going to be straightened out. One chorus we sang a lot was about abiding in the vine.

I found a new way of living,
I found a new life divine,
I have the fruit of the spirit,
I'm abiding, abiding in the vine.
Abiding in the vine, Abiding in the vine,
Love, joy, health, peace, he has made them mine,
I have prosperity, power and victory,
Abiding, Abiding in the vine.

It sounded really good, but it really said nothing about abiding in the vine. While the song majors on specific fruit, as in the fruit of the Spirit, that was not what Jesus was teaching His apostles about abiding in the vine. I also remember another version that was more hymn style, sung in some of the Pentecostal churches.

Abiding in the vine,
Abiding in the vine,
All the riches of God's life are mine!
Praise God, He put us here,
Never to leave; oh, we're —
Abiding, abiding in the vine.

These lyrics say that God "put us here," that is, in the vine, and that's absolutely true. He placed us in Himself (the vine) and that's where we are to abide!

For Jewish people in the first century, the symbol of the vine was very much about them. Scriptures from the Psalms, Isaiah, Jeremiah, Ezekiel and Hosea describe the Israelite people as God's vine. Interestingly enough, all the Scriptures that reference Israel as the vine are negative, referencing faith-lessness or punishment. In the time of the Maccabees, the vine was on the Jewish coins and it had come to be viewed as the national symbol. So when Jesus said that He was the true vine, their heads probably snapped up: they always believed that they were God's vine, and He was saying that He was the true vine, and they were branches? He had gotten their attention, and they were zeroed in and tracking on His words.

God and the Vine

Most see this illustration as a grapevine in a vineyard. The Greek word is vine, and most often referred to a grapevine, although it could be used of a different vine or plant. So I will use vine or plant interchangeably. We must see this just as Christ's Jewish followers would have seen it that final night. They had always seen the Father as the Vinedresser (the Greek word is more general, as in the cultivator or gardener); but they saw themselves as the actual vine or plant.

The Jewish people were disqualified from being the vine/plant because of three things. Firstly, they had failed to do what God wanted them to do; they went through the religious motions, even adding all kinds of extra motions (works) to perform. But their hearts were far from God; they did not abide in Him. Secondly, they were not being the blessing that God intended, in reaching all the nations. Thirdly they were rejecting Jesus Christ, instead of accepting Him by faith.

So the Lord Jesus Christ, God Incarnate, was becoming the vine/plant, and all people that plugged into Him would be fruit-producing branches in the New Covenant plant. The Gardener/Vinedresser was doing what was necessary for the plant to live, thrive and produce fruit. Father God was not willing to let the plant die; He brought the New Covenant that would make the plant eternal, and bring significant fruit. The actions of the Father, the Vinedresser, need to be interpreted in the context of switching from the Old Covenant failure (because of the Jewish people), to the New Covenant success (because of the Lord Jesus Christ).

Romans 11:17-23 – But if some of the branches were broken off, and you, being a wild olive, were grafted in among them and became partaker with them of the rich root of the olive tree, do not be arrogant toward the branches; but if you are arrogant, remember that it is not you who supports the root, but the root supports you. You will say then, "Branches were broken off so that I might be grafted in." Quite right, they were broken off for their unbelief, but you stand by your faith. Do not be conceited, but fear; for if God did not spare the natural branches, He will not spare you, either. Behold then the kindness and severity of God; to those who fell, severity, but to you, God's kindness, if you continue in His kindness; otherwise you also will be cut off. And they also, if they do not continue in their unbelief, will be grafted in, for God is able to graft them in again.

Paul expressed this dual concept well in Romans, using the olive tree as the plant. There was an Old Covenant time when being a bloodline Jewish person meant one was part of the plant. But in the New Covenant being a part of the plant depended upon the individual's faith in the Lord Jesus Christ. From the point of the cross on, Jewish and non-Jewish people could be part of the plant, based on their faith, or cut off from the plant, based on their unbelief.

People and the Vine

Each time Jesus referred to branches in this illustration, He was talking about people. Please do not jump to the conclusion that all of these people are Christians. Remember that Jesus is showing His disciples the paradigm shift from the Old Covenant plant, which had not worked because the Israelites failed to keep their hearts close to God, to the New Covenant plant, which would work based upon their faith in Him and abiding connection to Him.

Taking away branches. Jesus expressed that branches not bearing fruit would be taken away. The Jewish people of the Old Covenant were not bearing fruit, so the Father was taking them away. They had been God's chosen people for generations, but the fullness of time had come, and the covenant paradigm was changing. In the New Covenant all people, Jews and Gentiles alike, could be branches in the plant, if they accepted Jesus Christ by faith, and abided in Him. The natural consequence of this faith and abiding is the bearing of fruit.

Throwing away branches. The Jewish people who chose to reject Jesus Christ as their Messiah could not abide in the One who they did not believe. No abiding, no faith, no more being a part of the plant. Their fate was to dry up, then be bundled up and thrown into the fire. This sounds terrible, but remember Jesus came to the Jewish people and spent 3 ½ years presenting the truth and the word to them; but they rejected Him. It is also true that Gentiles who chose to reject Jesus Christ have no faith in Him, are not abiding in Him, and therefore are never a part of the plant.

Pruning branches. Some branches do bear fruit, and the Father does what He needs to, so that they can bear more and more fruit. The Greek word translated "prune" really means something closer to cleanse or clean. (KJV – purgeth; NIV – trim clean). God does what He needs to do to clean the branches so that they bear more fruit. This is why Jesus immediately assures His disciples that they are already clean because of the word He had spoken to them. It would be incorrect to assume that the works we do in bearing fruit are what qualify us to be a part of the plant. It is the cleansing we receive from Jesus Christ that qualifies us as part of the plant, and enables us to bear the fruit He desires us to produce.

So the Old Covenant illustration of the plant/vine had to give way to the New Covenant illustration, and the people/branches that rejected Jesus Christ/the vine were no longer a part of the plant. But the people/branches that accepted Jesus Christ/the vine were absolutely a part of the plant, cleansed by the word of Jesus Christ, and already producing more fruit.

> It means to be connected in such a strong way
> that an unbroken connection is maintained.

Abiding in the Vine

The word for abiding has at its root meaning "to remain." It is more than just being there. It carries permanence in the meaning, as in being in a close and settled union. It means to be connected in such a strong way that an unbroken connection is maintained.

To illustrate the strength of the connection: in the Roman Empire of the first century, they had leases, just like we do today. A lease has legal strength that affects the length of time, the cost, the conditions, etc. If there was a disagreement between the leaser and lessee as to the terms of the lease, and it was taken to court to break the lease, if the court decided the lease was to stay in effect, it would rule that "the lease and its terms would remain in effect (the Greek word abide). Not only is the "connection" supported by a written lease document, but the legal action and weight of the court makes it like double abiding.

A more practical illustration of the strength of the abiding connection comes to mind, when I work with computer components. If it's not wireless, I work with cables and connections. I have noticed that the simple plug-in cable can often come loose with very little pulling. It happens to me a lot. But some cable connectors plug in, and also have a little screw on each side of the plug in, that you screw in. As a result the connection is much stronger, and rarely pulls out. It abides.

Or if you are going to mount something heavy on the wall, you can use those fasteners that screw through the plaster board, and then when you screw the bolt in, on the other side of the plaster board some metal folds up and holds tightly to the inside of the plaster board. But it still is supported only by the plaster board, and I have seen those come loose, taking a piece of plaster board right out of the wall. A far better way to mount that heavy thing on the wall is to identify where the wood 2 x 4 stud is on the inner wall, and screw deeply into that wood. You rarely see that kind of wall-mount support come loose. The connection is supported, maintained and abides.

That's the way the disciples were to abide in Jesus: strongly connected and established in place. In an interesting way He double-commanded them: you abide in Me, and see to it that I am abiding in you. He told them that they couldn't bear fruit unless they abided in Him.

Jesus incentivized them with the promise of empowered prayer. By abiding in Jesus, and allowing His words to connect, settle and abide in their being, He promised that they could ask whatever they wished, and it would be done for them. Obviously, His words abiding in them would filter out inappropriate requests. With His words abiding in us, we freely seek first His kingdom and His righteousness, trusting that whatever worldly things we may need, He will provide.

He also reminded them of His love for them. Just as the Father had loved Him, Jesus also loved them. He simply reminded them to abide in His love. Connect with it; abide in it; bask in the warmth of it; rest in His wonderful love. In that final night He had given them commandments of love: the love flowing from God to them, their love flowing back to God, and their love flowing to one another. He had pure interaction with His Father, freely kept His commandments, and consequently abided in His love. So to, as His disciples had pure interaction with Him, allowing His words to abide in their hearts, they could keep His commandments, and consequently abide in His love.

Jesus made a beautiful and persuasive presentation of the how's and why's of abiding in Him. But He also pointed out that anyone that didn't abide in Him would be thrown away, dry up and be burned. How sad is the end result for anyone that rejects the Lord Jesus Christ.

Fruit of the Vine

The fruit can and does apply to many positive things that grow out of the life of Jesus Christ, and the lives of His disciples. Godly character is certainly fruit, like the fruit of the Spirit: love, joy, peace, patience, kindness, goodness, faithfulness, gentleness, self-control. Also, it is wonderful fruit each and every time we lead someone to the Lord Jesus Christ. The context around the Vine illustration is that of love, obedience and a successful prayer life. Those very things growing and increasing in the life of each disciple are manifestations of wonderful fruit. When referring to the fruit in the grape vineyard, one is speaking of the grape: the produce. Certainly godly character is good produce, and as the grape has the potential to reproduce the grape plant, so godly character has the potential to produce new Christians. Fruit in all these aspects is very positive, and I do not believe Christ intended that "fruit" be narrowly defined in this illustration. His disciples knew that any fruit stemming from Him would be the best fruit.

So He reminded them that without Him and by themselves, they wouldn't be producing any fruit. But with Him and abiding in Him, they would be the producers of the most wonderful fruit. And it is no accident that degrees of fruit production are spread throughout this illustration. Fruit, more fruit, much fruit. The intermutual connection of abiding in Jesus, and having Jesus abide in them would bring about the greatest production of fruit: much fruit. And that would all roll uphill, glorifying the Father, and proving the validity of their discipleship.

So the illustration of the Vine and the Branches painted a positive picture for the disciples: a picture of the New Covenant in the cross of the Lord Jesus Christ, and their productive role in it. The production of fruit is certainly important to the illustration. But for me, abiding is the most important concept: all of us, as His disciples, abiding in Him. That abiding entails depths of connecting and permanence in residing. People, we live and move because we abide in Him, so let's abide-connect-establish in Him, so that our living and moving produces the most wonderful fruit!

John 15:16 – You did not choose Me but I chose you, and appointed you that you would go and bear fruit, and that your fruit would remain, so that whatever you ask of the Father in My name He may give to you.

On a personal note, this passage in John chapter fifteen has a very special meaning. When I was seventeen years old, I was with a youth group that made a trip to a small town in Oregon to minister to the community. We were working in teams of two, going door to door, trying to lead people to salvation. We had special services each evening at one of the local churches, and were seeing some results, with young people coming to Jesus. Late one night, after the church service was over, I was out walking and talking with God. I had been reflecting on John chapter fifteen about the vine and the branches, and I was pressing into being really connected with and abiding in Jesus. With the sincerity and impatience of youth, I was crying out to God to let me know what He wanted me to do for Him in my life. He suddenly and clearly spoke to me! It was not audible, but it was clear and strong inside of my head. He wanted me to be a pastor, and He pointed me directly to John 15:16: "Ye have not chosen me, but I have chosen you, and ordained you, that ye should go and bring forth fruit, and that your fruit should remain; that whatsoever ye shall ask of the Father in my name, he may give it to you"(KJV). It was my calling, and from that moment on, I knew God wanted me to be in full time ministry. I made it my goal to be in ministry for the Lord, from that time on, and every time I read about the vine and the branches, I always read through verse sixteen, to remind myself that God called me and ordained me. I am His minister; I will abide in Him by faith and I will bear fruit for Him.

Chapter Fifteen

WORKS, WORKS, GREATER WORKS

Greater Works than these shall we do!

John 14:12 –Truly, truly, I say to you, he who believes in Me, the works that I do, he will do also; and **greater works** *than these he will do; because I go to the Father.*

The very idea that we who believe in Jesus Christ will do the kind of works that He did is awesome, breathtaking and exciting. At one point Jesus sent out seventy of his disciples, in pairs, to proclaim that the kingdom of God had come. They performed miracles in His name, with people getting healed and demons getting cast out. When they reported back to Jesus, they were excited and full of joy at the signs and wonders that happened in His name, but through their hands. We all feel the same way. If we pray and people are healed; if miracles happen at our hands, it is awesome! And on the final night He told them that they would do "greater works." They must have been thinking: Whaaaaat?

The idea of us doing "greater works" than Jesus does is a challenging one. I have seen two different reactions to the concept.

It can't be literal. Some Christians respond with doubt. How can anyone do greater works than God Himself? It can't have a literal meaning, because there's no way a sinful human could do greater works than Jesus. Maybe it has a symbolic meaning.

Look at me! I'm greater! Others respond with excitement and zeal. "I can do greater things than Jesus did!" But their focus slips into taking some of the glory, and their reputation and what they can do become the focus, instead of God's kingdom and righteousness being the focus. Neither of these reactions helps us walk in the "greater works" that the Lord intended.

As a Bible College student I had the opportunity each year to serve an internship at a local church, as part of my pastoral training. Each pastor was to impart the wisdom of his ministry experience to me, so that I could be a better pastor in the future. In my first internship, as an assistant pastor, the pastor gave me a strong caution about praying for people to be healed. He told me that the gift of healing was not to be desired because it could lead to pride and a fall. He told me that as a young pastor, he had prayed for people to be healed, and many miracles were happening. But he told the Lord to take the gift of healing away from him, because there was too much danger that he would take the glory for himself, and he did not want it to distract from his pastoral ministry. So he stopped having people healed when he prayed for them. I remember him telling me, "You don't want that gift of healing. Run from that as fast as you can." Both then and now, I didn't agree with his advice. I believe we can do whatever the Lord wants us to do, including miracles, without taking the glory and falling into self pride. I believe God wants us to do the works that Jesus did, as He walked this earth.

I remember when my wife and I had the privilege of being part of the special choir for a Kathryn Kuhlman Crusade in Seattle, WA. This gave us the opportunity of seeing everything from the wings of the stage, and afterward we were altar workers, praying for people who were accepting Christ, or recommitting their lives to Him. It was staged very professionally and presented somewhat dramatically, but everything we saw and experienced was Biblical. She did not exercise the gift of healing. Instead she spoke words of knowledge or words of wisdom about who God was touching, healing, and calling. She would speak a word and then wait for the individual identified to come forward. If the person did not come out of the audience, she often would keep praying and narrowing it down, until she identified the individual and called them forward. She rarely prayed for or touched someone who came forward; she had platform staff to handle that. They would have some people share their testimony. We did see several people miraculously healed through the week. It was a very different way for people to receive miracles, or come to the Lord, but it did work for many. Signs and wonders that resulted in people getting saved; just like in the Gospels and the Book of Acts.

Several years later, when I was an Associate Pastor, on staff at an Independent Assemblies of God church in the Seattle area, the Lord was teaching me the key concept of using our imagination as the creative expression of faith. On a number of occasions when people came forward for prayer to be healed, the Lord used me in praying the prayer of faith, and people were healed. Two stick vividly in my memory; one newly married woman healed from uterine cancer; one year-old baby healed from significant heart deformity. Both healings were verified by further testing and diagnosis from the doctors (I have always believed that if someone receives a miraculous healing, they should get verification from the medical community).

I share these stories to let you know that I believe we should do miraculous signs and wonders and healings, just as Jesus did, so that many more come to believe in Him and partake of the salvation of the cross. The death of Jesus on the cross ushered in the New Covenant, and His atoning work provides salvation and healing. We should do the works of Jesus. BUT…greater works?

Truly, truly – This was a unique way that Jesus had of introducing certain statements He made. The Greek words are a transliteration of an Aramaic word: aman. We use the word all the time these days: amen. When we end a prayer, or when we express agreement with something that has been said in the teaching or sermon, we say "Amen." In a different way, Jesus used the term twice at the beginning of a statement. This use of the term seems to be unique to Jesus. It certainly was meant to mark out the following words as solemn, true and important. We believe that every word spoken by the Lord is very important, but we also want to acknowledge the added emphasis that Jesus intended. It is only in the gospel of John that Christ is shown speaking the word twice at the beginning of a statement. It is almost like the Lord is using this introductory "amen, amen" as an oath, like the Old Testament phrase, "As I live, says the Lord." It means much more than simple agreement. It means something like this: "Listen up! I stake My life and My word on this concept."

It was totally new doctrine for them!

He who believes in me — The apostles still struggled with understanding the deity of Christ. Jesus wanted them to grasp that He was in the Father and the Father was in Him.

It is difficult for us to understand fully the Godhead, and how we have one God, eternally existent in three persons: the Father, the Son and the Holy Spirit. Though we have trouble understanding it, we fully accept it and believe in it. That Jesus Christ is the Son of God, and God the Son, and that He was fully God and fully man at the same time is also difficult for us to understand. But we fully accept it and believe in it. The apostles struggled with these concepts, and they were struggling to fully accept it and believe in it. It was totally new doctrine for them! Jesus had just made several statements making it clear that He and the Father were one, and that the works that the Father did and the works that He did were one and the same. Philip spoke up and said, "Show us the Father, and it is enough for us." Jesus said, "Have I been so long with you, and yet you have not come to know Me, Philip? He who has seen Me has seen the Father." Jesus was leading them into their next step of faith – faith in Him and faith in the New Covenant – full belief in the Lord Jesus Christ. When that was accomplished they would do the works that He did. "If you believe in Me, you will do the works that I do."

The works of Jesus. So what are the works that Jesus does?

John 14:10, 11 – Do you not believe that I am in the Father, and the Father is in Me? The words that I say to you I do not speak on my own initiative, but the Father abiding in Me does His works. Believe Me that I am in the Father and the Father is in Me; otherwise believe because of the works themselves.

Jesus expressed that He was in the Father and the Father was in Him. He made it clear that everything He spoke was what the Father wanted, and the works that He performed were the works of the Father, just done through Him. Christ was not operating independent from Father God. I think that Jesus stated this concept so often because He could see that we humans tend to separate the doings of the Godhead. He wanted us all to understand that the Father and the Son and the Holy Spirit only do what they all want. There are no separate egos or agendas within the Godhead. Jesus was doing and saying only what the Father wanted done and said.

In John chapter five, Jesus starts out by healing the lame man at the Pool of Bethesda. Because it was the Sabbath, the Jews objected to the healed man carrying his pallet and also that Jesus had performed the healing. There is a lot of discourse about Jesus doing what His Father wanted him to do, and the Lord cites four things bearing witness of Him: John the Baptist (v. 33), the Father (v. 37), the Scriptures (v. 39) and the very works that He did (v. 36).

The works that Jesus did were not done to distinguish Him from the Father and the Holy Spirit, but to help us all see what the Father and the Holy Spirit wanted done. If I put it in a formula, it would read: works of the Father = works of the Son = works of the Holy Spirit. The works of God, as manifested by Jesus, were a witness that was to help people believe in Him.

John 6:30 – So they said to Him, "What then do You do for a sign, so that we may see, and believe You? What work do you perform?"

The works of Jesus did include the miracles, healings and casting out of demons that he performed. He performed each of those signs to help the people who were healed and delivered. For people who had hearts to believe, these works did bear witness and help their belief. But for the ones who rejected Him, who opposed Him, the signs and works didn't change their minds. They had seen Him perform the miracles, but still asked Him to justify His teachings by more signs and works. They were not going to change. They would not believe.

When John the Baptist sent some of His disciples to ask Jesus if He was the Messiah, Jesus pointed to the healings and miracles that were being done; and He also said that the poor had the gospel preached to them. He was making it clear that part of His works that proved He was the Messiah was the preaching of the gospel to the poor.

All the preaching, sayings, signs and wonders that came from Jesus were to help the people believe in Him, and respond in faith to the greatest work of all: New Covenant salvation through His death on the cross. Those were the works that Jesus spoke of doing, and those are the works that we who believe in Him will also do. The sayings, signs and wonders that we do in the name of the Lord Jesus Christ will lead people to salvation in Him. Those are His works that we do.

Greater works – The Greek here is literally "greaters." Greaters than these will he do...Greaters than the works Jesus did we will do. Before the cross and the New Covenant in His blood, His disciples were already proclaiming the kingdom of God, as well as performing signs and wonders in His name. So the signs, wonders and preaching were the works that Jesus did, and said that those who believe in Him would also do.

But what are the greaters?

Because I go to the Father – This is the key to really defining what the greater works were to be. The disciples performed signs and wonders before Jesus was going to the Father. Only by dying on the cross for salvation did Jesus accomplish the ultimate goal of God: that man could be saved from sin and restored to full relationship with God. It was then that He went to the Father. So the greater works that we are to do have everything to do with the spreading of the gospel message and the resulting people who accept Jesus.

You will do greater works than I do, because I go to the Father. As Jesus told them just before the Day of Pentecost: "You shall be my witnesses in Jerusalem and Judea and Samaria, and to the uttermost parts of the earth." And in the Great Commission He directed them: "Go and make disciples of all the nations, baptizing them in the name of the Father and the Son and the Holy Spirit."

On the day of Pentecost Peter preached the message and 3,000 men accepted Christ. When Peter and John ministered healing to the lame man at the Beautiful Gate, and Peter preached the message, 5,000 men became believers in the Lord Jesus Christ. As you follow the apostles in Jerusalem and Judea, the message, accompanied by signs and wonders resulted in more and more people becoming Christians. The apostles and other disciples spread the message of the gospel throughout the Roman Empire and beyond, and more came to be believers in the Lord Jesus Christ. Through almost 2,000 years since the crucifixion of Christ, the followers of Christ have ministered the gospel message, with signs and wonders accompanying them, and millions have become believers in the Lord Jesus Christ. These are the greater works that Jesus spoke of. Every time you and I minister the gospel message of the Lord; every time we pray for God to perform miracles, and He does, we are fulfilling the words of our Lord on that final night. Greaters, people! Greater works! That's what the church has been doing throughout this church age.

Chapter Sixteen

YOU DON'T KNOW IF I'M COMING OR GOING

(You don't know about My going or coming)

Even though Jesus had been telling the disciples of His impending trials in Jerusalem, they didn't seem to understand or accept that. Now it was down to the final night, and for the disciples, it would seem that the sky was falling in. So Jesus stated His "going and leaving" again and again, trying to get through to them; to forewarn them; to prepare them. In that process He laid out His "coming again," so that they would know what to do and whom to rely upon. I broke this down into a five-part chronology: 1-Jesus going to the cross; 2-Jesus coming back in the resurrection; 3-Jesus going into heaven to the Father at His ascension; 4-Jesus coming back in the indwelling presence of God; 5-Jesus coming back in His 2nd coming. I have placed these final night Scriptures into one of these five parts, but you will see that the parts are intertwined in several of the verses. Let's take a look.

Going to the Cross

John 13:33 – Little children, I am with you a little while longer. You will seek Me; and as I said to the Jews, now I also say to you, 'Where I am going, you cannot come.'

John 16:16-22 – A little while, and you will no longer see Me; and again a little while, and you will see Me. Some of His disciples then said to one another, "What is this thing He is telling us, 'A little while, and you will not see Me; and again a little while, and you will see Me'; and 'because I go to the Father'?" Jesus knew that they wished to question Him, and He said to them, "Are you deliberating together about this, that I said, 'A little while, and you will not see Me, and again a little while, and you will see Me'? Truly, truly, I say to you, that you will weep and lament, but the world will rejoice; you will grieve, but your grief will be turned into joy. Whenever a woman is in labor she has pain, because her hour has come; but when she gives birth to the child, she no longer remembers the anguish because of the joy that a child has been born into the world. Therefore you too have grief now; but I will see you again, and your heart will rejoice, and no one will take your joy away from you.

Jesus knew that within hours He would be separated from His disciples, arrested, tried, crucified and buried. For about three days they would be separated from Him. They could not come where He was going; they were not strong enough to be with Him for the arrest and trial; they could not die on the cross with Him. It was only a little while, but they would weep and lament and grieve. They would be fearful, ashamed and bitter. Their Messianic paradigm would come crashing down. It was because they had not accepted what He had been warning them about. They were not opening their eyes to see the bigger picture.

I want us to open our hearts to identify with and understand the disciples. We may think that they should have had a full grasp of what was happening. After all, they had walked with Jesus for 3 ½ years, seen His signs and wonders, heard His teachings. Surely they knew who He was and what He was doing! He had told them plainly that He would go to Jerusalem, suffer and be killed at the hands of the elders, chief priests and scribes, and be raised after three days! Surely if we had been there, we would have understood and accepted what was happening; maybe, but probably not. I think we would have been just like them. Get the picture. Back when Jesus had asked them, "Who do you say that I am," and Peter made the marvelous declaration: "You are the Christ, the son of the living God," it was a high point. Surely the disciples were ready for the New Covenant paradigm. And yet Jesus had then stated plainly to them that He was going to suffer, die and rise again after three days. They didn't want to hear it. Peter actually pulled Jesus off to the side, and rebuked Him, saying, "God forbid it, Lord! This shall never happen to You." Peter was the one speaking, but all the disciples shared his position and beliefs. They had a paradigm: the Messiah was returning to establish God's earthly kingdom, in which they would live and be blessed. This belief was so ingrained into their beings, that they could not and would not accept the reality of the New Covenant paradigm. You can read all about it in Matthew 16:15-23. But the Cross of the New Covenant was about to happen, and Jesus was communicating everything He could to help them through the transition.

So Jesus let them know that they would have pain and anguish, and that they would weep, lament and grieve, because He was gone, He was dead, they were separated from Him. But He would return from the dead, and all the negative would be replaced by joy. Like a woman travailing in birth, they would suffer pain, but afterward would have joy, like a mother with her newborn.

A few months before I graduated from Bible College, our second daughter was born. I remember her birth for the pain and anxiety of the labor: pain for my wife and anxiety for me. We lived about 1 ½ hours away from the military hospital where she was to be born. My wife had gone into painful labor, and I was driving our little Honda Civic (1200cc engine) as fast as I could, spurred on by my wife's gasps and cries of pain, as each contraction came more rapidly. I actually remember being on the freeway and passing all cars, on the left shoulder, going about 85 miles an hour (yes, that little car went that fast, at least once!). Ahead I saw that the left shoulder suddenly disappeared, because of some underpass. So I coached another couple of miles an hour out of the little car, and swung back into the left lane, just barely ahead of a large Chevy! At this risky driving behavior, my wife reached over and squeezed my leg painfully, and said: "You're doing good honey." She was in so much pain that she could put up with my anxious and crazy driving. When we got to the hospital, she barely got into the delivery room in time. I had to fill out some quick paperwork, but even though it was quick, I missed the birth of my second child. That whole process was full of pain and anxiety, but, oh the joy, when the baby girl was there! It helps me understand why Jesus used that as an example of what His disciples would be going through in the next three days; and an example of the joy coming.

Coming back after death, hell and the grave (The Resurrection)

John 14:18, 19 – I will not leave you as orphans; I will come to you. After a little while the world will no longer see Me, but you will see Me; because I live, you will live also.

Jesus would rise from the dead and be with them again. He would be alive, and back with them! Orphans (Greek: fatherless) have no one to look after them or provide for them. But Jesus reassured them: they would not be fatherless; they would not be abandoned; they would have joy in the morning! Jesus made it crystal clear: I will see you again, and you will see me. One more thing he said to them: a little while. This devastating separation would not last indefinitely. It would only be a little while (maybe they would be reminded that He had told them He would rise again on the third day).

Going into the heavens (The Ascension)

John 13:1-4 – Now before the feast of the Passover, Jesus knowing that His hour had come that He would depart out of this world to the Father, having loved His own who were in the world, He loved them to the end. During supper, the devil having already put into the heart of Judas Iscariot, the son of Simon, to betray Him, Jesus, knowing that the Father had given all things into His hands, and that He had come forth from God and was going back to God, got up from supper, and laid aside His garments; and taking a towel, He girded Himself.

John 14:28-31 – You heard that I said to you, 'I go away, and I will come to you.' If you loved Me, you would have rejoiced because I go to the Father, for the Father is greater than I. Now I have told you before it happens, so that when it happens, you may believe. I will not speak much more with you, for the ruler of the world is coming, and he has nothing in Me; but so that the world may know that I love the Father, I do exactly as the Father commanded Me. Get up, let us go from here.

John 16:4-7 – But these things I have spoken to you, so that when their hour comes, you may remember that I told you of them. These things I did not say to you at the beginning, because I was with you. But now I am going to Him who sent Me; and none of you asks Me, 'Where are

You going?' But because I have said these things to you, sorrow has filled your heart. But I tell you the truth, it is to your advantage that I go away; for if I do not go away, the Helper will not come to you; but if I go, I will send Him to you.

John 16:28 – I came forth from the Father and have come into the world; I am leaving the world again and going to the Father.

John 17:11-13 – I am no longer in the world; and yet they themselves are in the world, and I come to You. Holy Father, keep them in Your name, the name which You have given Me, that they may be one even as We are. While I was with them, I was keeping them in Your name which You have given Me; and I guarded them and not one of them perished but the son of perdition, so that the Scripture would be fulfilled. But now I come to You; and these things I speak in the world so that they may have My joy made full in themselves.

But in the New Covenant Jesus would not be with them in His physical body.

Jesus was also looking beyond the phase of His incarnation. The disciples had been with Him, physically, for around 3 ½ years. He would also be with them, physically, for around forty days. They were very dependent upon His physical presence. But in the New Covenant Jesus would not be with them in His physical body. The new paradigm of the New Covenant would come into full operation on the Day of Pentecost, when the Holy Spirit would be in them. The Feast of Passover, and the subsequent Day of Pentecost that happened 50 days later, were Old Testament type and shadow of the New Testament reality of the Cross and the indwelling of the Holy Spirit. That is why the paradigm shift was over a period of fifty days. Jesus also wanted His disciples to start getting prepared for the shift from physical dimension relationship to spiritual dimension relationship. So He referred several times (at least seven times) to the reality that He was leaving the world and going to the Father. On that final night, this was the second leaving that Christ referred to. The first was His leaving to go to the Cross. The second was His ascension, after He had appeared to them over a forty day period in His resurrected body. From Acts:

Acts 1:9 – And after He had said these things, He was lifted up while they were looking on, and a cloud received Him out of their sight.

Coming back to be inside of you
(The indwelling presence of God)

*John 14:1-4 – "Do not let your heart be troubled; believe in God, believe also in Me. In My Father's house are many dwelling places; if it were not so, I would have told you; for **I go to prepare a place for you.** If I go and prepare a place for you, I will come again and receive you to Myself, that where I am, there you may be also. And you know the way where I am going."*

John 14:5, 6 – Thomas said to Him, "Lord, we do not know where You are going, how do we know the way? Jesus said to him, "I am the way, and the truth, and the life; no one comes to the Father but through Me.

John 17:24 – Father, I desire that they also, whom You have given Me, be with Me where I am, so that they may see My glory which You have given Me, for You loved Me before the foundation of the world.

For His disciples, from the moment on the Day of Pentecost when they were baptized with the Holy Spirit, from that moment on, the Holy Spirit was in them. God was in them. Jesus Christ was in them. Whether the indwelling happened for them at the moment Jesus died on the cross, or by the Day of Pentecost baptism fifty days later, God was in them. And for us, participants in the New Covenant, from the moment we accept Jesus Christ as our Savior and Lord, the Holy Spirit is in us; God is in us; Jesus Christ is in us. His disciples had worked with the paradigm that had been around for over 1,400 years: God's presence was represented by the Tabernacle or the Temple. But this new idea, this New Covenant indwelling presence of God; that God Himself would be inside every one of His followers; that was a magnificent idea! But it was so different from the old way of experiencing God's presence that Jesus had to forecast and establish its wonderful reality. In the New Covenant, we would be with Jesus forever, because He is in us forever. That's why Jesus could conclude the Great Commission with the assurance of His presence:

Matthew 28:20b – and lo, I am with you always, even to the end of the age.

When Jesus died on the cross and ushered in the New Covenant, His ultimate authority in the spiritual dimension was clearly "stamped" again, and He paved the way to our new functioning in the spiritual dimension with all of His position, authority and power. We are seated with Him at the Father's right hand in heavenly places. With Him within and always present, there would be no more absence, no more separation; only "togetherness with God" forever. On that final night Jesus showed all of us that the way was in Him and His presence. "I am the way and the truth and the life."

Coming back at the end of the age
(The Second Advent – Second Coming of Christ)

John 14:1-4 – "Do not let your heart be troubled; believe in God, believe also in Me. In My Father's house are many dwelling places; if it were not so, I would have told you; for I go to prepare a place for you. If I go and prepare a place for you, I will come again and receive you to Myself, that where I am, there you may be also. And you know the way where I am going."

The idea many people see here is that Jesus returned to heaven and is preparing a place for us. When we die, or for those still living when the 2nd coming of Christ occurs, we will be taken to our special place in heaven (mansion). So we are assured that Jesus will come again. And this was clearly stated by the angels, when Jesus ascended into heaven.

Acts 1:11 – This Jesus, who has been taken up from you into heaven, will come in just the same way as you have watched Him go into heaven.

But there was also a more immediate "spiritual dimension" meaning. The Father's house may refer to heaven. But in John 2:16 Jesus used the phrase in referring to the temple He had just cleansed of animals, coins, money changers and sacrifice sellers. "Stop making my Father's house a place of business." And Paul indicates the household of God is the church of the living God (I Timothy 3:15). Spiritually speaking, Jesus was saying that in His church there are many places/positions that His people are to occupy. He was going to prepare and make ready the place for His people to occupy. The Greek word for place may also be translated space or region or realm. When He died and was resurrected, He fully achieved the plan of salvation for mankind. Consequently He has the position of ultimate power and authority in the spiritual dimension, and His people also have this position of power and authority because of what He did. He defeated death, hell and the grave and has been given the position of authority and power far above all rule and authority and power and dominion in the spiritual dimension. And that is our position too! Jesus fully functions in the spiritual dimension because He died and was resurrected. That's where He is, and that's the place He was preparing for His disciples, so that they could function in the spiritual dimension.

We know that at the end of the Church Age, Jesus will return, and we will be with Him in the new heavens and new earth, wherein dwells righteousness. Jesus prepared His disciples for His goings and His comings, and after the panic and fear of the separation caused by His death on the cross, they allowed their Old Covenant paradigm, not just to shift, but to be smashed, so that they could operate fully in the New Covenant paradigm. Thank you Lord!

IN CLOSING

Jesus has been with us and within us for all of our Christian lives. There have been those precious times when the Lord has said something special to us. We can picture how it must have been to be in a small group with Jesus, and have Him speak for several hours. And we can picture how awful it must have been for His followers to be separated from Him when He was arrested, tried and crucified. But, oh, those wonderful truths He imparted are so precious.

Jesus made it clear to them, again and for all time, that He was God; not just a rabbi; not just a prophet; not just a human Messiah. When they saw Him, they were seeing God. When they heard His words, they were hearing the voice of God. When they called out His name over their lives or in their prayers, they were calling out the formal covenant name of God: the Lord Jesus Christ. And through the indwelling of the Holy Spirit, and His activities, they had God in His fullness; which included God's words, God's will and God's purpose. God would be with them and in them forever!

From the first shocking event of washing their feet, to the concluding prayer proffered to the Father about their unity, the disciples were challenged to have the best relationships of any human group or organization. Love one another to such a degree that who washed whom's feet would never be an issue. Quite to the contrary, they would press into being slaves for one another, and serving each other in such a way that their own self interests wouldn't even be an issue. His disciples were to have such a unity that the world would be rocked with their message and their lives. They would first be called Christians in Antioch, because people who saw and heard them would be seeing Jesus Christ.

They were reminded of just how badly some people would respond to the Lord and to them, as they watched the son of perdition, the unclean one, reject Jesus and go off to betray Him. But they were also encouraged by the interactions of the Lord and their under-leader, Peter. Simon Peter was so human! It seemed like he was a living illustration of how weak and how strong human character could be. But in all of it, Jesus still loved and guided him. And Jesus loved them and would guide them, through the thick and the thin.

They were given the outline of the shift from the Old Covenant to the New Covenant. More than that, they were convinced of the surpassing value and glory of the new paradigm. It would help them see the deeper meaning of glory: not just fame, shine, brightness and recognition, but the ultimate glory of His death on the cross. And maybe for the first time they began to glimpse what peace the New Covenant paradigm offered to all mankind; to all who believed in and received their Lord Jesus Christ. Sure, persecution and trouble might come their way; and it might cost them their lives, even as their Saviour had laid down His life. But the surpassing value of the opportunity of peace between God and every individual human would outweigh any negative.

They would connect and plant themselves so firmly in Jesus that their fruit for the kingdom of God would explode and overflow. They would never be God, like Jesus was. But with God inside of each one of them, greater works would flow out into the world, and within just a few generations there would be millions of followers for their Lord Jesus Christ.

Yes, Jesus would be going away; gone and separated from them by His death on the cross. But how quickly He would appear again; their risen Lord! And more importantly, by the indwelling of the Holy Spirit, He would come again and be with them forever.

It was the Final Night. And Jesus loved them to the end – and then beyond – forever.

I want you, as a Christian, to benefit from the Final Night teachings. Going to church does not make us Christians. Hanging around Christians does not make us Christians. Performing religious acts does not make us Christians. Only by accepting the free gift of eternal life from Jesus and inviting Him to come into our hearts and lives can we be saved and partake of the relationship and inner dwelling that He has taught us.

If you have done this, you have the necessary communion with His Spirit to partake of these precious truths and priority teachings. If you have not, I invite you now to become a Christian. Pray this prayer right now, and you will be born again and begin establishing your personal relationship with Jesus.

"Dear Jesus, thank you for dying on the Cross for me. Please forgive my sins and come into my heart and life. I step down from the throne of my heart, and ask you to sit there. I will abide in You, as you abide in Me. Help me walk in Your unity with my fellow Christians, so that I can live the abundant life you want me to live. I accept that I am saved by faith and grace. I love you Lord. Amen."

ABOUT THE AUTHOR

Reed Tibbetts has served for over twenty-three years as an ordained pastor and teacher, and is currently serving as one of the elders of VLife Church in McKinney, Texas, where he ministers as a prophet and teacher.

An honored and decorated disabled veteran of the Vietnam War, Reed is a graduate of Northwest University of the Assemblies of God. Over the many years he has pursued the goal of handling accurately the word of truth, and has developed a reputation as a guardian of apostolic doctrine (the teachings of the apostles).

Through the years Reed has written and printed many teaching notebooks in the churches he has served, but only recently has he turned to the writing and publishing of books for the greater body of Christ.

Reed lives in Princeton, Texas with his wife of forty-six years. They have three adult children and four grandchildren, all of whom are faithfully serving the Lord in their respective local churches.

AUTHOR CONTACT

Reed has written several other books about the successful Christian life. If you would like to contact him, find out more information, purchase books, or request him to speak, please contact:

Allegro Ministries
470 San Remo
Princeton, TX 75407
yahovah3@gmail.com
214 724-7541

Allegro Ministries is a non-profit corporation, formed by Reed and his family, recognized as a 501(c)(3) by the I.R.S. It exists for the purpose of spreading relevant teachings to the church of the Lord Jesus Christ, so that more and more people can live the brisk and lively Christian walk. If you would like to contribute to the ministry, please send your offerings to the above address, and thank you for your giving.

www.ingramcontent.com/pod-product-compliance
Lightning Source LLC
LaVergne TN
LVHW051104080426
835508LV00019B/2049